Dear Reader

Please help save our Children — May
God Bless You + Yours — Love
                    Joil Mathis

# No Place to Run, No Place to Hide

## By

## Esther J. Mathis

This book is a work of non-fiction. Names and places have been changed to protect the privacy of all individuals. The events and situations are true.

ISBN: 1-4033-8376-6 (e-book)
ISBN: 1-4033-8377-4 (Paperback)
ISBN: 1-4033-8378-2 (Dustjacket)

Library of Congress Control Number: 2002095981

This book is printed on acid free paper.

Printed in the United States of America
Bloomington, IN

1stBooks - rev. 12/11/02

This is a true autobiography about the life of an abused child, growing up in the 40s' and 50s'. The reader will come to see how the author must deal with the loss of her mother and the impact of foster care. Then she goes on to endure trauma at the hands of an abusive adopted mother.

Joe'l and her sister Rose were very young when their mother passed away. Their father was unable to care for the two small girls, so he sent them to several foster homes. Later they were sent to an orphanage. After years of being shifted from one relative to another, the girls ended up in the home of their mother's sister, Aunt Sue. Shortly after their arrival the abuse began. Daily extreme physical, mental and verbal abusive conditions were bestowed upon Joe'l, the younger of the two girls, but surprisingly never on the older girl Rose. Joe'l endured eight long years of this horrifying treatment, but, with the Lord's help, she survived.

This book will take you through those terrifying years, and allow you to witness first-hand the cruel and awful effects of abuse. It will lead you out of the abusive system and into the adult life of Joe'l. It also will allow you to see that an abused child can overcome tremendous obstacles and blossom into a loving, caring wife and mother without fulfilling the expectation that "An abused child will always become an abusive parent". She and her sister are living proof, as they have not succumbed to becoming abusive parents.

No Place to Run, No Place to Hide, will fill you with fear, horrify you with graphic details, and slowly warm your heart with the triumphant outcome. The author, Esther

Joe'l Mathis, is today a mother and a grandmother. She is a member of the Broadlands Community Church, a member of the Louisiana Council of Child Abuse, and was a volunteer for the program entitled "Welcome Home". This program assisted new mothers in dealing with the stress of coping with the daily struggles a mother of a newborn must face.

As author of No Place to Run, No Place to Hide, I hope and pray you can assist with the publication of my book and look forward to hearing from you in the near future.

Thanking you very kindly in any you can assist,

Sincerely,

Esther Joe'l Mathis
186 Joelle Mathis Road
DeRidder, Louisiana 70634

# **<u>Acknowledgements</u>**

I would like to give thanks to the following people who have made this journey possible

Lori Haymon; for giving me insight and purpose to write it all down and get it out.

To Vivienne Miles-Perkins; for all her expert advice with my computer problems, and setting me straight, getting me back on track when I thought all was lost.

To Gerri Richardson, for suggesting the title of my work.

To Richell Clossener, for helping me with the beginning stages of my work.

Johnny and Linda Johnson; as they headed me in the right direction to Sandy Burk.

Sandy Burk; for spending countless hours editing my work, making sure everything flowed in correct order.

Rose Campbell; my sister, for helping me to remember and achieve the beginning goals of this work.

Donna, Therese, and Timmy; for bearing with me through trail and error.

To Brandy J. Cantrell; for designing my cover and for all her expertise advice.

To all who have encouraged me not to give up over these many years. I appreciate and Thank you.

# <u>Authors Note</u>

To my readers: Please, if you are ever in a situation where you are involved, witness, or have knowledge of a child being abused in any manner, please get help. You can call your Preacher, Teacher, Doctor, Social Worker, or your local Prevent Child Abuse Number, or please call the Prevent Child Abuse Hotline: 1-800-348-KIDS. It shouldn't hurt to be a child.

**Thank You**

# Poem

## To My Sister

*The Author of this book lived this abuse*
*No one listened, No one believed*
*No one cared, but I knew*
*Because I lived it with her,*
*I am surprised she is alive today,*
*God have had to been watching over her,*
*All through those years.*

*From*
*Your Sister Rose*

# <u>A Dedication</u>

This book is dedicated to my sister "Rose" who
Stood by me throughout the horrible ordeal,
And who still stands by and believes in me.

To my three wonderful children,
Therese May,
Billy Joe,
And
Donna Dee

Who have honored me by calling me their
Mother.

# A Sisters Testimonial

I remember my Aunt Sue used to beat my sister when we were small. There wasn't much I could do about it. Every evening when Joe'l came home from school, my aunt would take her up to the attic and beat her for no apparent reason. Sitting at the kitchen table, I could hear her beating my sister. Over the years, it seemed as if the beatings went on for eternity.

My sister says that she didn't hate her, but I did. My Aunt didn't want my sister. She only wanted me. Actually she favored me, but I don't know why. She abused me in other ways than physical. For example, I remember her dictating a letter for me to write. The letter, which I was forced to write, faulted my father for my mother's death. Also when Aunt Sue was married to her first husband, Uncle Bob, she made me go in front of a judge at her divorce proceedings and lie. I was told to tell the judge that while I was in the bathroom taking a bath, Uncle Bob peaked through the bathroom door at me. I lied for her in court, which enabled her to get the divorce.

When I became 18 years old, I decided to leave Aunt Sue's and take Joe'l with me. I didn't want to live there anymore. In those days at eighteen, a child could leave home, but my sister was only 16 years old. I took her with me anyway, because I knew Aunt Sue would have killed Joe'l if I had left her there.

I remember the day one of our cousins came for a visit to see how we were doing. He didn't like the looks of the house. It was as though we were living in a morgue. We told him she kept us in the house all of the time and how mean she was to us. Our cousin said he would call our father and get him to come get us.

I had to plan our escape. I planned on taking a suitcase with a few clothes in it to the corner grocery store, after I informed the owners what we were doing. They allowed us to keep the suitcase in their store until we were ready to leave. We told Uncle Sammy we were going to the store and we would be right back. Instead, we caught a cab and went to my cousin's apartment. Meanwhile, Aunt Sue knew we had run away, so she had the police out looking for us. I used to think I could have been arrested for kid-napping my own sister, but I didn't care as long as we could get away from Aunt Sue. When our father came, we had to go to court. The Judge awarded my sister and I back to our father, and we moved home to New Orleans.

All those years of hell, especially for my sister, were finally over. My Aunt had to be really sick, a very evil person, in my opinion. She had two sides to her. When she was in public, she was very nice, but with us she was really mean.

By, Rose
Campbell

xiv

*This is a photograph taken of myself and Rose at the home of my mother and father on Cleveland Street in New Orleans.*

*The Autobiography of an Abused Child*
*Esther "Joe'l Mathis*

# PREFACE

Back in the 1940's and 50's, such topics as abuse whether physical, mental, verbal, and/or sexual abuse were not publicly known in our society as they are today. If you were to mention such, people would turn a deaf ear. These kinds of things just didn't happen. But, they did, and they are still prevalent to this day. Child abuse, which happens every day, has become a more recognized issue than ever before. Not being loved or wanted by your relatives is an unhappy dilemma for any child, and there are more than three million children reported as victims of child abuse and neglect every year. Even in this day and age, our justice system fails so many children. It still doesn't work for the child. It is as though the authorities must be a witness to the abuse as it is actually happening before they can take action, step in, and remove the child before it is too late.

When society catches an abuser, what is it the lawyers always use on behalf of their defense? "An Abused child grows up to become an abusive parent." No, not **ALL** abused children do. Ask yourself, "Why would you want to deliberately put your own child through the horror of the pain, fear, and suffering that you yourself had to endure?" When a parent who has been an abused child uses that abuse as justification for abusing children, he or she is the abused. Sure the abuser must know there is a better way not only for himself/herself, but also for his/her children.

As I began to write my story, I became very angry, shaky, and emotional. I questioned myself about whether or not I really wanted to remember all of this. Not realizing how upsetting it would be, I discovered I could not continue writing for any length of time. Finally, being determined, even though it was not easy, the more I wrote, I found the less it hurt. Writing it down and getting it out, has been a tremendous healing experience. It has taken me several years to remember as much as I have. So much had been blocked out of my mind all through the years. I am a 63-year-old widow, the mother of three, grandmother of six and great-grandmother of one. After 55 long years, I am telling my story about eight long, terrifying years of child abuse.

It is my hope and prayer that my story will help inspire at least one other abused person to overcome anger and frustration by turning them into love and understanding. With the Lord's help, an abused person can become a better person. With Him ALL THINGS are possible. God's unchanging love and protection does enrich our lives.

# Chapter 1 "Mother and Father"

My mother passed away from tuberculosis on July 25, 1944. I vaguely remember her, but I do remember she was so sick she couldn't cook for us. She taught my sister, Rose, how to open a can of soup, pour it into a pot, and then set it on the stove to heat. This way we could have something to eat.

Although my memories of my mother are few, I've been told she was very sweet, loving, and a kind, gentle lady. One of my cousins revealed that mother had a beautiful singing voice, and she loved to play the piano. Once my mother auditioned for a radio program and won a small radio as her prize. From the pictures I have of her, I know she was very pretty. She had black hair and black eyes, and she was tall and thin. We also have pictures of my sister and me dressed alike in pretty little pinafore jumpers, as mother loved to dress us alike. She would place a curling iron on the stove to heat and curl our hair into ringlets.

My mother's grandparents immigrated from Canton, China and settled in Denver, Colorado, in the early 1800's. Her great-grandfather, became the first mayor of "Chinatown" in Denver. He earned a chair of honor in the Central City Opera House. His story is written in the <u>Colorado Profiles of Men and Women Who Shaped the Centennial State</u>. My great-grandfather and one thousand or more men, whom he recruited from his native China, laid the steel rails to complete the Kansas and Pacific Railroad. This was the first railroad in Denver. A portrait of him and several of his men is engraved in stained glass at the entrance of the Opera House. After immigrating alone, my great-grandfather sent for his wife in 1873. They had three children, a girl and two boys. The girl was my grandmother. Even today, several of my relatives still live in Denver, but I have never met them.

My father's family immigrated from Italy to the United States and also settled in Colorado. I don't have as much information about them as I do my mother's family. I have been told that as teenagers, my father and several of his brother's hopped freight trains going to South Louisiana. Other relatives in my father's family remained in Pueblo, Colorado. And although I have heard of them, I have never met them either.

My sister and I were born in New Orleans, Louisiana, and we lived there for the first few years of our lives. The house next door and several down the block had the old time pretty wrought iron fences and gates, which are traditional around New Orleans. Our house was situated in the older section of town, on Cleveland Street, just off of the famous Canal Street. All the rooms were built one right behind the other, "shotgun" style. The house consisted of a living room, an old fireplace built in the wall, one bedroom, a small kitchen, and a bath. Furniture was very scarce; the living room held a couch and one rocking chair. In the bedroom we had one bed, a small dresser, and a cot, which my sister and I shared. All the windows had wooden shutters.

One vivid memory of my early childhood involved the shutters. When I was very small, my head got caught in one of the blinds in the shutters and I couldn't get it out. Some people passing by stopped to push my head backwards through the blinds. I never tried that stunt again! Another time I stuffed a wad of cotton up my nose. There it stayed, until my mother got some help to retrieve it. Living with us was my mother's brother, Uncle Sammy. He was tall and thin with black hair and black eyes, just like our mother. His good friend, Carlo, came quite often to visit our little family. We girls dubbed him "Uncle Carlo." He allowed us girls to sit on top of his stomach and punch him in the nose until it bled. We thought we were big and tough, but we really didn't hurt him. He was just pretending. Being quite small, we really couldn't have hurt a flea.

Another vivid memory occurred when I was about four years old. I developed scarlet fever and was hospitalized for about three weeks. Since I was quarantined, father brought ice cream and gave it to the nurses to give to me. No one could come to visit. I felt all alone, and frightened. I was in a room all by myself, in a youth bed with the side rails up. Everything was all white and sterile. Before the nurses could enter my room, they had to put on white sterile gowns, gloves, and masks. As I sat by the window looking out watching the rainfall, I remembered my mother's words, "rain drops are like tin soldiers marching as they splashed down in neat rows." Her words brought comfort and helped pass the time away. I missed all of my family terribly.

While I was still quite young, my mother became ill with tuberculosis. For some reason I remember that during her illness there were air raids. Back in the late '30's and early '40's during World War II, the civil defense system had cities practice air raid drills, which were called black outs. Whenever the air raid siren sounded, we turned all the lights out in the house. My father would scoot us under the bed first, and then he would crawl under with a flashlight in hand. This was to prepare us in case any enemy planes happened to be flying over our city. Then, the siren sounded again giving the all-clear signal. As I was too young to understand, I often wondered why my mother never came under the bed with us. Later, I realized she was too sick to move out of that bed.

Rose remembers the day they were taking her to the hospital. She turned around as they were wheeling her out of the house and waved good-bye to us. Mother didn't want to go to the hospital; she had tried all different ways to get well but to no avail. Our mother was only 33 years old when she passed away. Back then there was no known cure for tuberculosis. Rose remembers her funeral, but I do not. Standing next to Aunt Sue at the funeral, Rose remembers Aunt Sue crying out, "don't put her in there" as mother's coffin was lowered into the ground. Aunt Sue was mother's oldest sister. When mother died, Rose was six years old and I was four. Not understanding death, we only knew she was gone, and we would never see her again.

Our father worked the midnight shift as the headwaiter at the Roosevelt Hotel in New Orleans. He waited tables in what has become know as "The Blue Room". He enjoyed his job tremendously, always very jolly and friendly to everyone he met. This is where many celebrities would come to perform their acts. He became known to quite a few of his customers over the years. They began asking for him by name. Some of the celebrities he served were Bob Hope, Frank Sinatra, Teresa Brewer, Rose Mary Clooney, Perry Como, Red Skelton, and Patti Page.

Our father was short with dark complexion and had lots of curly black hair. He loved to play the harmonica, making it sound just like a freight train whistle. My sister and I have brown eyes just like our father and black hair just like our mother. He was always the happiest while fishing but he also loved watching baseball games, especially the World Series. His other favorite past time was going to the racetrack and betting on horses. There he spent a lot of his time. Every weekend when he was off from work, he'd go fishing. I remember asking him when he caught a bunch of crabs why he put them in the bathtub with salt on them. I thought surely they were already salty! I loved eating grabs and still do, although I don't get them very often anymore. Also, I have pleasant memories of watching my father shave. Back then men used a mug and a brush to make the shaving cream. He would rub the brush around the cup holding the shaving cream and add water to make it lather. He would put the shaving cream on my face. I always thought the cream smelled so good and clean.

Not having any idea what to do, or how he could raise two small girls working the hours he did, after mother passed away our father enrolled us into a Catholic Orphanage. This must have been a hard decision for him; at least, we could be together and be watched over.

**Psalms 121:8 "The Lord shall preserve thy going out and thy coming in from this time forth, and even for evermore."**

# Chapter 2 "The Orphanage

The Annunciation Convent was huge. Consisting of red brick with two stories, it took up the two blocks it sat on. The playground was lined with large trees that surrounded the whole building. The front steps were high and steep up the main front entrance. All the nuns were dressed in the traditional long black habit of their order. They were very different from how they are dressed today. They wore their rosary wrapped around their waists like a belt. As they walked, their long robes made a swishing sound, and their rosaries swung along with their stride. There were nuns everywhere, in the main halls, in the bedrooms, in the kitchen, in the schoolrooms, in the chapel. I can't remember any of their names; it was so long ago, and so much has happened since then.

There were a lot of children there for one reason or another. All the beds were neatly lined up side by side in rows of five or six deep. We had clean linen, and everything was spotless. The floors were all shining with wax. Rose and I slept right next to one another. We clung to each other feeling very insecure. We stayed close to each other not trusting anyone other than ourselves. What kind of place was this? We weren't certain why we were there or why our father hadn't come back for us. Often I would stand in a corner crying for hours on end. Obviously we felt neglected, unwanted, and abandoned. Shortly following the loss of our mother, we were faced with the trauma of being left by our father in this place.

Each day we arose early, at daylight. The nuns came in clapping their hands to awaken us. Every morning we attended church (Mass) before anything else. After we came back, breakfast was served. It was usually oatmeal that had gotten cold while we were in church. Juice and milk were served with the oatmeal. The dining room table was very long, with all of us children sitting on either side. One of the nuns sat at the table on the very end. There were a lot of nuns to help with all the children.

After breakfast, we marched off to class in rows of twos. The nuns taught us manners, cooked for us, taught us our school lessons, and served as our guardians. We first studied our Catechism, and then did our regular school work. Our school desks were the old fashioned wooden kind, with the desk on top where we did our work. The lid rose up to put our schoolbooks inside. Right under the seat was a small shelf to put our satchel. If by some mischance, we misbehaved, we were struck on the knuckles with a ruler. The nun would approach the desk. She would instruct us to lay our hands on top of our desk, "and then WHAM!" This stung and hurt, but it was not nearly as hurtful as what was in store for me in the near future.

We were allowed visitors on weekends, but father seldom came. Anxiously we awaited his arrival. Although he did come occasionally, his visits began to dwindle. It took a while, but finally our situation became very clear to us. This was an orphanage, and we were placed here because no one in our family wanted us. On visiting days, when one of the other children's names were called to go home, we felt very miserable, unhappy, totally rejected, and ignored. Father left us there and got on with his life. Even so, our very good friend, "Uncle Carlo", came quite often to visit. He'd take us out for a few hours, treating us to ice cream cones and snow cones. We happily and eagerly

7

looked forward to his visits. I don't remember anyone else coming to visit us the whole time we were there.

If no one came to visit us, which was quite often, we pulled K.P. duty. We peeled potatoes, shelled peas, snapped beans, washed dishes, hung out clothes, and swept floors. Everyone helped with the chores to pass the weekend. When finished with the chores, we were allowed to go outside and play with the other children who didn't get to go home either.

While at the orphanage, I became ill. While ill I would often dream of an airplane that would nose-dive and crash. Right after it crashed, I would awake with a horrible headache. The room and ceilings were spinning, and I could hardly hold my eyes open. Being very nauseated, I was terribly sick. Noises made my head feel like it was going to explode. So I wouldn't disturb the other children, the nuns moved my bed into a room close to theirs. They watched me around the clock, taking turns to help me recover. I learned later in life that I suffered an ear infection, the first of many more.

We were treated very well, receiving three square meals a day and clean beds. We attended church and school and studied our Catechism. Both of us made our first communion in 1946. We were learning to adjust.

**Psalms 119:105 "Thy word is a lamp unto my feet, and a light unto my path."**

# Chapter 3 "New Home, The Windy City"

After three and one half years, it became evident we couldn't stay there forever. Our father came and took us out of the orphanage. He began switching us back and forth between relatives. This wasn't easy as these families had children of their own to raise. One of the families had four children and one had eight. Aunt Kit and Uncle Al, on my mother's side, had four children. Uncle Anthony and Aunt Rita, on my father's side, had eight children. We would have made six and ten. Back then times were very hard.

First, father tried leaving us with Uncle Al and Aunt Kit. But, beings they had children closer to our age and some younger it became too much on Aunt Kit. Besides, I had more inner ear infections and stayed sickly most of the time. Even though Uncle Al was studying to become a Dr. there wasn't much he could do for me. During the time we lived with them, one of there young sons was burned on an electric heater. Then we all caught the mumps, everyone one of us. Aunt Kit had her hands full; so it was decided it might be best if we were sent to stay with Uncle Anthony and Aunt Rita.

While we were staying with Uncle Anthony and Aunt Rita, we often walked to a park that had a swimming pool. We swam most of the day about every day. My uncle and aunt both worked, so that left us in the care of their eldest daughter, who at the time was barely 16. Having to watch over nine children is a big job, especially as active as we all were. I remember at nighttime, we captured June Bugs, which we all called lightening bugs. We kept them in a jar and at night took a string or thread and tied it to one of their

9

back legs. While holding the end of a string, we'd let the poor bug fly around in a circle. We also played many games of jacks. If there were enough dimes to go around, we would go to a matinee movie one Saturday a month, which was really a big treat. I believe it was called the Famous Theater, just off Marigny Street. A coke was a nickel back then. While we were staying at our Uncle Anthony and Aunt Rita's, Aunt Sue contacted our father. She wished to adopt my sister, but did not want me. Aunt Sue and Uncle Bob had been married several years, and did not have children of their own. Our father considered this; his answer was that she would have to adopt us both. Also, after my mother's death, Uncle Sammy had moved to Chicago to live with Aunt Sue and Uncle Bob. At first, she would not agree, but father insisted and, wanted us girls to be together. When we learned this, we were elated; possibly, here was some place we could call home. What an adventure awaited us! Plus, we were going where it snowed! A new city, a new life was in the making for us. I thought I'd have a chance, and Aunt Sue might perhaps, learn to like me. Unfortunately, I began to realize later I was mistaken' I had misjudged her.

So in 1947, we moved from South Louisiana to the windy city of Chicago, Illinois, where Aunt Sue and Uncle Bob made their home. At first things went rather smoothly as we got settled in and all. The house was situated in a very quiet, respectable neighborhood. Living in the city, we had a very small backyard; the front was mostly concrete. The famous Brock Candy Company sat right across the street from our house. From all the aromas of the candies cooking, we would have visions of all the goodies being made. It was in operation twenty-four hours a day. Every year Uncle Sammy painted the house a light green; this was Aunt Sue's favorite color. There were two bedrooms downstairs, a living room, kitchen, one bath, a small pantry, and a small back porch. Uncle Sammy occupied the first bedroom, Uncle Bob and Aunt Sue, the second one. Also, there was a formal dining room used only for holidays.

The house was always spotless; nothing was ever out of place. Aunt Sue would always say, "Cleanliness is next to godliness." The living room was like a mausoleum. All the chairs and the couch were draped with sheets or plastic. We only used the living room at Christmas time. The house was very dreary looking with the windows shut and all the curtains drawn at all times.

A pair of curvy stairs led up to the attic. The front of the attic was turned into a bedroom for us girls. The ceiling of the attic came to a high pitch, with the walls slanted on each side. We had twin beds with an apple crate for a dresser, which sat in between our beds. The top shelf was Rose's; the bottom shelf mine. This was where we stored our underclothes, of which mine were very few. These were the only furnishings in our room. The attic consisted of two rooms. The back room was a storage area. Uncle Sammy hung a long rod on which to hang our clothes.

The furnace and the wringer washing machine were situated in the basement. We heated with coal and had old-fashioned radiators for heaters. Someone had to keep coal shoveled into the furnace at all times, especially when the weather turned below freezing. In the wee hours of the mornings, the fire turned into ashes and then burned down or out. It became considerably cold in the house, especially in the attic.

A few evenings, Aunt Sue and Uncle Bob took us out on sightseeing tours around the city. Sometimes, they treated us to an ice cream soda, a float, or a banana split. We would drive past the Wrigley's Spearmint Gum Factory, take a ride down to see Lake Michigan, or just drive around looking at all the various skyscrapers. We didn't have many pleasures, but these stand out in my mind. Not long after this, terror set it, and there were no more outings.

*1 Peter 5:7 "Casting all your care upon Him, for he careth for you."*

# Chapter 4 "Torture Begins"

A very short time later, the effects of not being wanted began to be felt. It was as if I were to become Aunt Sue's target to hopefully be driven to insanity. Torture was my horrifying treatment. I received whippings and lashings for no apparent reason on a daily basis. As a child I discovered the meaning of total fear, fear from the *beatings* and fear for my *life*. It seems child abusers have the need to take their anger and/or frustrations out on defenseless innocent children. They grab any deadly weapon within their reach. Without reason, they literally beat, stomp, punch, lash, bruise, slice, and throw their victims. A way to rid themselves of an unwanted child is to beat the child almost to death. The child wishes for death, then there would be peace. No more hurting. It seems they don't care how much harm they inflict on their tiny little victims. It hurts!

Even though I do not have the bleeding, bruises, whelp marks and broken bones anymore, I still hurt. The very tiptop of my head has been tender, even until this day. My heart palpitated rapidly each and every time she approached me with whatever weapon she readily had in hand. I was in a state of panic. My abuse felt she must be in control. I viewed her as having the power of the Devil. She was the dominant one; she ruled.

For her favorite deadly weapons, Aunt Sue would use a thick belt from her old treadle type Singer sewing machine. This stung and as it cut deep into my flesh. Her high heel shoes, of which were like long, thin spikes, came crushing down and left small lumps over the top of my head. (It's a wonder these things didn't stunt my growth.) She used a

**2x4** inch thick board that was approximately 2 ½ feet long; that left large, broad marks all over my head, thighs, and backside. As I was forced to sit in a kitchen chair from daylight until dark, I was conveniently at her mercy. It's a miracle that I didn't have a fractured skull. I was confused and disheartened, wondering what I had done to deserve this type of treatment.

She used anything she could grab, such as ketchup bottles or drinking glasses, which she broke over the top of my head. Once when she did this with the ketchup bottle, we didn't know which was ketchup and which was blood. It was all mixed together with glass in my hair. Ketchup and/or blood ran down my face. This particular episode took place while on a trip to visit my Aunt Kit and Uncle Al in New Orleans. They and their family witnessed this horrible event. I remember it was at night, and I ran out of the house, into their front yard and hid among the bushes. I was scared, humiliated, and terrified. They and some of their children came out looking for me. Although they witnessed this horrible scene, the abused never stopped. Neither they nor anyone else cared enough to become involved.

*Psalms 55:22 "Cast thy burden upon the Lord and He shall sustain thee."*

# **Chapter 5 "Grammar School"**

We enrolled in a nice grammar school. It was a long wooden building that housed grades one through eight. There was heat in most of the rooms, but none in the basement. This is where we ate our lunches and shivered. Not long after enrolling, I was chosen to be the bell girl. I rang the bell to begin and end each recess. I also rang it for lunchtime. It became my responsibility each year I attended until I graduated from the eighth grade.

We got along rather well with the children from our school. We made friends, but we really never had any close friends. One year for our Christmas play, my music teacher chose me to sing the lead part for "O Holy Night." We had to try out for each part; she said I had the highest soprano voice, soft and sweet. I was thrilled and quite privileged. Rose was the only member of my family who came to watch me as I performed.

There were other pleasant memories from these school days. I remember at recess and at lunch I always played on the monkey bars. I loved to swing on the high-flying bar that went around and around, higher and higher with each turn. It was fashioned similar to a maypole. I gained momentum with my feet as I ran and pumped, holding onto the bar. My feet would rise up and I would swing higher and higher into the air. It was fun and very exhilarating. In about the fifth grade, I entered a Spelling Bee contest, never thinking I would have the possibility to win, but win I did. These types of experiences motivated me and helped me retain my self worth and dignity. They were priceless to me.

Perhaps because Aunt Sue wanted me to fail, I made good grades. This made her angry. I would sit and write my homework over and over, giving me something to do besides just sit. The drudgery of sitting in that chair day by day was all I had to look forward to in addition to the dreaded, unending beatings. I made good grades by drilling information into my head, using repetition. Being very hard on myself, I wanted to make good grades for me also.

From the time I was eight until I was eleven years old, I needed glasses. Aunt Sue said I only wanted them so I could look like the other children. She didn't think I actually needed them. When the teachers wrote assignments on the blackboards, I had to go up to the front of the room and put my nose right against the blackboard. This was the only way I could see what had been written, as I was very near-sighted.

After numerous attempts and *years* of teacher's notes, she finally took me to be fitted with a pair. They looked like little ole' granny-type glasses, small and round, but I didn't mind. I will never forget looking through the first pair. Seeing all the lovely green leaves on the trees waving in the breeze with the sun radiantly shining through was like a whole new world! Everything finally looked so clear. While in the house, I was never allowed to wear them. She feared they would break when she walloped me in the face.

We walked the eight blocks to and from school in all kinds of weather- snow, sleet, rain, and/or sunshine. I liked the snow falling onto the palm of my gloves. The flakes were so pretty; the weather was cold and crisp. We gathered snow, from parked cars, and shaped it into snowballs. As we walked, we threw them at each other on the way to and from school. Sometimes, the school custodian let the water hose run overnight. The next day when we got to school, there was a neat ice rink. I never learned to skate on two skates, but I could manage on one. Rose could skate on two skates quite well. This was good exercise, very enjoyable and lots of fun, especially when one of us fell down!

Because our school did not have a cafeteria, we packed cold lunches. We made peanut butter and jelly sandwiches, and sometimes, luncheon meat and cheese sandwiches. Across the street from school, was a small sandwich shop that served hot dogs, hamburgers, candies, cookies, and cokes. Aunt Sue gave Rose spending money, but she never gave me any. Whenever my sister had money left, she would buy me a hotdog. As seldom as I got such treats at home, I made that poor hot dog last until the entire lunch hour was nearly over. I took very small bites, savoring the taste of each morsel.

Because of all the crying from the lashings I received, I developed frequent sties on my eyes. I was sent to school this way. The children were afraid of me and ridiculed me. Once, when a sty covered my entire eye, I sat in school with that horrible thing on my eyelid. It was so heavy that I could not hold my eye open. After it burst, the teachers tended to me. Also, boils came up on the outside of both my legs. I cried from the pain of walking everyday back and forth to school while my legs throbbed. Aunt Sue had begun to put black slave on them until they came to a head and burst. That was so painful I thought my legs were going to fall off. I developed the boils from wearing high top boots all those years.

The only times I remember being allowed to wear a dress was at Christmas, at Thanksgiving and at graduation from grammar school. They were Rose's handed down dresses, but to me they were just as pretty as new dresses. When I graduated from grammar school, no one from my

17

*Esther J. Mathis*

family came. All of my classmate's parents and their immediate families were there for them. Rose didn't come either. I just walked around watching all the other children making plans to go different places with their families. As I walked home I was sad, but very proud of another accomplishment.

*Philippians 4:13 "I can do all things through Christ which strengtheneth me."*

# Chapter 6 "Verbal Abuse"

Verbal abuse almost always goes along with physical abuse. During the time I lived with her, Aunt Sue drilled these words into my head: "Your parents didn't want you' nobody wants you. Your father didn't want another girl; he wanted a boy. You are no good; you are ugly and stupid. The world would be better off without you. Your face is just like a monkey's. You have no brains; you are an ignoramus. You won't do well in school or anything else; you can't learn. You will never get married; no one will ever want you. If you do marry, your children will die. You are a nuisance, a pigeon-toed, worthless individual." All these comments that were inflicted on me were very derogatory. I had to listen to them repeatedly through out the years. I would flinch and try to slide under my chair whenever I heard these words.

The verbal abuse really made me feel very unwanted by everyone concerned. I began to become timid, shy and meek, drawing into myself. I reasoned that Aunt Sue didn't have any children and, therefore, she probably had no maternal instincts. This could explain why she didn't know how to treat us any better. I was scared and intimated. I never talked back or complained. As these circumstances were beyond our control, Rose and I never really discussed why this was happening to me. We had a dismal outlook on life; there was never a kind word or praise from her for either of us. This mental and emotional abuse shocked, saddened, silenced, exasperated, and amazed us. The reality of it was too much for our youthful comprehension. Aunt Sue never talked or spoke to me as a normal person speaks

19

to a child. She'd bark orders at me: "Come here, do this or do that, go to bed, eat all of your food." She never used full sentences, only short to the point words and phrases.

My curfew was always around six or six-thirty every evening. But at least there I could be safe for a little while. I was out of sight and out of the way. Once in bed, while there was still plenty of daylight; I would read as many classics as I could: Little Women, Little Men, Heidi, Tom Sawyer, Black Beauty, Huckleberry Finn, and Alice in Wonderland, etc. These were books she had bought for Rose. Going on the adventures with the characters in the books was my escape into a fantasy world. Another escape was of different foods I would like to eat. If Aunt Sue came up to check on me, I hid the books under my mattress and pretended to be asleep.

*Psalms 147:6 "The Lord lifteth up the meek; He casteth the wicked down to the ground."*

# Chapter 7 "Fear"

Fear takes control and lives with the child forever. I am extremely grateful, thanking God every day for my mere existence. By His Grace I have lived through the fear and feel it is a miracle I survived. My evasive abuser hit where the whelps or marks and bruises were not visible. She would hit on the top of my head where my hair covered up the marks or on my backside and thighs where clothing covered up the evidence. Taking her revenge out on me, she was relentless, cruel and unmerciful, making sure not to break any bones.

One day while slicing vegetables at the kitchen sink, Aunt Sue claimed she could see me blinking my eyes. This was not allowed! With a spontaneous reaction she just turned around and with that paring knife slashed me on my wrist. Scaring the life out of me, the blood spurted up to the ceiling. The bleeding was difficult to stop. To this day I was the scar because I received no stitches or medical attention. Aunt Sue patched it up herself. Sometimes I tried to fight back, but I was too small. I tried kicking her in the stomach, but I missed and kicked air. This just angered her more, and she'd scream, "I'll teach you how to fight back!" As I struggled to get away, she'd hold me down while beating me harder. Often she used the 2x4 and beat me on my thighs and the top of my head. Several times she threw or forcefully pushed me down the attic stairs. I bounced down that curvy set of stairs, and unknowingly injured my tailbone. I didn't know it had been broken. That circumstance may have contributed to the fact that I had trouble carrying my children. Both pregnancies were difficult, and I had several miscarriages.

My face was another one of her favorite targets. She would strike me in the face mostly with her hand, making my nose and mouth bleed. It seemed I always had a swollen lip and blood bruised nose. I don't believe my nose was ever broken, though. No amount of crying or pleading would stop her. She would stop when she was ready and not before. I felt trapped, tormented, and overwhelmed by the erratic, enraged and uncalled for actions, which became a daily event. While I was being tormented, I inwardly cried out, "I wish, I could get away; if only I had someplace to go."

*John 14:27 "Let not your heart be troubled, neither let it be afraid."*

# Chapter 8 "Starvation"

Starvation, (going to bed without supper night after night) is another form of abuse. On every birthday she would send me to bed without supper and greet me with, "This is your birthday present." Before she'd send me she would mix up what she called a "milk shake". This consisted of one raw egg, a small amount of sugar, and vanilla mixed into a glass of milk. I drank this down in place of supper. There was always plenty of food in the house.

Aunt Sue was a very good cook; she served lots of oriental dishes. Two of my favorite were chop suey and sweet and sour pork. For breakfast we either had cream of wheat or French toast. In order to eat, I always had to ask permission. Sometimes she had baked cream puffs that would melt in my mouth. When the weather was right, she made divinity candy. She tantalized me with a very small amount of these delicacies. Many times she bought cakes from the bakery. My favorites were the kind that had the cake in the middle, with lots of cool-whip on the sides and top. If this was one of the times I was allowed any, she'd cut a very thin slice for me, as though she couldn't spare more than that. This was my only slice, while everyone else, ate his or her fair share of the whole cake. Often times I would just watch while everyone enjoyed dessert.

I was allowed only one helping per meal. Aunt Sue would prepare my plate. If I was still hungry after I cleaned my plate I just stayed that way. Not being allowed to choose my food like other children, I was proud of what I did receive. She always told me I should be thankful someone took me in and fed me while the children overseas were starving. Well I wasn't like those children, but every now and then I'd wonder, "Am I?" There were times she'd cook food that made me sick. Tripe for example tasted awful, especially when cooked with tomato sauce. Periodically, we were taken to the dentist. At one appointment, I fainted as soon as we entered the office due to hunger.

One day we had hamburgers for supper. For some reason I couldn't eat all of mine. I guess my poor little stomach couldn't hold a big hamburger. So, Aunt Sue saved it for me. She put it into the refrigerator and took it out at the next meal. I had to eat it cold. The cold greasy meat didn't settle too well on my stomach, and I threw it up. That was not the thing to have done. I had to eat what I had thrown up and finish the cold hamburger meat. This and a glass of water were all I had for days and days, until I finished that piece of meat.

One of my cousins, Michael, came from New Orleans for a visit during the summer. He was probably eleven or twelve years old. This was a horrible scene for him to have witnessed. He never came for another visit, ever. Today he is a prominent physician.

*Matthew 4:4 "Man shall not live by bread alone; but by every word that proceedeth out of the mouth of God."*

# Chapter 9 "Aunt Sue and Uncle Bob"

Aunt Sue held a good job as a Licensed Practical Nurse at one of Chicago's most prestigious hospitals. On the job she was very kind and gentle to her patients. Working at a hospital for many years, she very was highly respected by her colleagues. She was a small woman, but much bigger than I! She had coal-black hair that was always curly. It looked like the wind kept it swept away from her face. Her eyes, black as coal, shot fire out from them whenever she came after me.

Uncle Bob was an engineer for the Baltimore and Ohio Railroad. He was a big, tall man who had lived on a farm in his boyhood days in Missouri. His blondish white hair was thinning, his eyes were light blue. He was very nice to us, never spanking or raising his voice to us. Whenever the abuse got too much and he couldn't stand it anymore he disappeared from the house. Either he would go for a drive or walked down into the basement. When he thought there was peace again, then he would return. He was good at making little things with his hands, like birdhouses and such. For our first Christmas he made each of us a very small jewelry box. I still have mine. Why he never became involved with the beating and lashings, I'll never know. Being over six feet tall he was big enough to have beaten her up five times over. But, I do know he had a soft heart and probably would not harm anyone. They were both well-educated middle class, gainfully employed, well-dressed and seemingly intelligent people. There is no evidence in her background, which I have found, that she herself had ever been mistreated. All the things she did to me were inexplicable.

Once we took a trip to Uncle Bob's family farm in Macon, Missouri. He drove the entire way there and back. It was a very pleasant trip. His mother and father, who were still living on the farm, were quite elderly and very kind. We had the nicest time, sleeping on the softest beds with lots and covers. For breakfast his mother cooked bacon, eggs, homemade biscuits with milk gravy, homemade butter, fresh cow's milk, and jellies, which she, herself had canned. To me this was a FEAST! I was served a second helping. I had never seen as much food as she placed on that table at each meal. We girls even rode horses, something we had never done. Uncle Bob and his father took us squirrel hunting. As we walked through the tall stalks of corn, the stalks were way above our heads. To keep up we had to stay in the rows, as neither of us could see over the high corn stalks. This was the only time we ever met his family. In this environment, Aunt Sue was always her sweet self and seemed as if nothing was amiss.

At home she was on her own turf. She ruled if something was white and she said it was black, her word was gospel. Even if that something was white, it was black. We didn't cross her. She always said she had eyes in the back of her head, meaning she could see anything I did. Of course, out of fear, I didn't do much of anything. If I even blinked my eyes and she didn't like it, she'd beat me. Being terribly aggressive, she was the only one with authority in the house-a brutal psychotic compulsive maniac. I never knew from one day to the next what awaited me. But, I could be certain that a couple of beatings a day were in store for me no matter what. We were never allowed to express our opinion on anything. Children should be seen and not heard.

I had a lot of things building up inside over the years that I wanted to voice, but of course I kept them to myself.

The hairstyle we wore was one she fashioned herself. She would take a kitchen chair outside, position us down in it, place a big bowl on top of our heads, and cut our hair around the bowl. She'd say, "Now, you have a bowl hair cut!" Our hair, which was black and very straight, was cut into a very short pageboy, way above our ears. I hated my hair cut like that, but of course there was nothing Rose or I could do. Years later, I let my hair grow way down my back, letting it get as long as I could stand it, trying never to cut it.

I was never allowed to help with household chores. Maybe she thought I might break or steal something. She said she never could trust me. Rose dried supper dishes and dusted. I never wondered why she never loved me, as I always knew it was as plain as the nose on my face, that she hated me. Feeling like I was a burden to her all those years, as though I was in the way she was trying her best to get rid of me any way she could.

One winter Rose caught pneumonia. Aunt Sue called a doctor; he came regularly and tended to her for about two weeks. These were the days when doctors made house calls. Rose says Aunt Sue never told her what she had until after she was well. I was so scared my sister would not get well and I wouldn't have her anymore.

*Psalms 46:1 "God is our refuge and strength, a very present help in trouble."*

# **Chapter 10 "Two Different Personalities"**

Aunt Sue knew exactly how to avoid the police; she evaded taking me to the hospital or doctor so as not to be reported. Oh yes, the neighbors complained for years; they called the police time and time again. They reported the yelling, screaming, and pandemonium going on in the house next door. Whenever the police came out to check the situation, they always called before they came to make sure someone was home. Well, this was a dead give-a-way. My abuser had time to clean up any mess and restore dignity; in the law's eyes, nothing appeared to be happening. Her secret was kept hidden behind closed doors. Naturally, when they came in to question us, we were instructed to lie: "Nothing out of the ordinary is happening here." But, yet, my heart was pounding and I was shouting within myself, "Please help us; don't leave us there, take us with you."

Rose and I never laughed, as there never was much to laugh about. We were never allowed to play with one another. Other children laughed and played together enjoying themselves, but not us. Our world was so full of hatred. We were never happy children, just sitting in those kitchen chairs every day. Our lives were very dull; it was a struggle to live day-to-day as we were emotionally drained. Of course, my sister didn't have to sit as long as I did. She could get up every now and then; she had much more freedom than I. Although I was never allowed to play like normal children, I did play on the playground at school. This and walking to and from school were the only physical exercise I had, other than ice-skating. After finishing my homework, I was made to sit with my arms folded across my chest, often from daylight to dark I just sat there. This way my aunt knew where I was at all times. The 2x4 she used was always in easy reach, as it lay on top of the radiator, right next to the chair in which I sat.

There were times I was ordered to memorize Bible verses. If I was unsuccessful in my attempt to recite the verse word for word, I was rewarded with a lashing. She didn't allow me to call her Aunt Sue, I was instructed to call her by her married name, "Mrs." I was not a bad or rebellious child nor hard to manage, that I should deserve this type of treatment. I did my best not to provoke her and I always tried to be on my best behavior. She was not demented, nor was she an alcoholic or drug abuser. But she was excessively brutal. She used physical force, violently inflicting deliberate painful injuries, leaving me with a bruised, bloodied body. Flying into rages, she turned her hatred onto me.

Most abusers have two different personalities. One personality is that of love and kindness, the other hateful and mean. Outside of our home, Aunt Sue was a completely different person. To others she seemed loving, kind, cordial, nice and friendly. Behind closed doors she became an abusive, adamant, obsessive, insufferable, degrading, and sinister being.

I feared it was if I were being punished for crimes I didn't commit. My sister or I never sought psychiatric counseling. Our healing later in life finally came through prayer.

***Psalms 40:1 "I waited patiently for the Lord; and he inclined unto me, and heard my cry."***

# Chapter 11 "Rose"

My sister Rose was a very good artist. She loved to draw, either sketching or copying the comic book characters such as Popeye, Olive Oil, Whimpey, and Sweet Pea and some of the characters from Li'l" Abner and Daisy Mae. Also she loved to draw muscle men such as Superman, Batman and Robin, Little Lulu and Dick Tracy were two more of her favorites. Once, she copied a picture of our Lord Jesus in the Garden praying just before he was to be crucified. After drawing the picture she would paint it, the results were simply beautiful. Also, she sketched and designed clothes. Rose could have gone on to become an artist if she had tried. I believe this was my sister's way of keeping her sanity. Whenever Aunt Sue beat me, if Rose voiced her outrage, I received more lashings for her outbursts. While she drew, she became so engrossed; she shut out the scenes around her.

This kind of life was no picnic for my sister either; I believe she felt terribly tormented by the scenes she had to witness. I know she had a lot of rage building up inside of her, as she was helpless to help me in any way. She may not have bore the scars, bruises, and whelps that I did, but she silently cringed from the suffering she knew I had to endure. All she could think of was a way to get us out of there, before it was too late. She had a plan going on in her head, but it would take years before she could put that plan into action.

Aunt Sue dictated letters for Rose to write to our father, telling him how much **WE** were loved, how much fun **WE** were having playing in the snow, and how many pretty clothes she bought for us. She painted a beautiful picture of a cozy, happy home. Along with the letters, she sent snapshots. She would take us outside and make us pose for the pictures. She instructed us how and where to stand in the snow and to act like we were throwing snowballs at one another. Portraying us as having a good time, she insisted we smile. These photo sessions didn't last long, but were a nice reprieve from just sitting. Then it was back to the chair, back to the same old routine.

Aunt Sue always bought new dresses for Rose, but none for me. I wore Rose's hand-me-down dresses, for which I was grateful. To me they were beautiful. Most of the pictures she sent were of Rose posing in all her new clothes, and of the house in which we lived. Father had no idea what was really taking place. He believed the pictures and the letters told it all. Years later we learned that our father had been sending us birthday and Christmas cards along with money in the cards. To our knowledge, we never saw the cards or the money. In 1948 our aunt and uncle legally adopted us. Father agreed because; he believed we actually were being treated well. At least one of us was.

*Psalms 91:11 "For he shall give his angels charge over thee, to keep thee in all thy ways."*

# Chapter 12 "Jesus Loves Me"

Church and School were my only release. To keep up appearances, we were allowed to attend Sunday School and Church at a Lutheran Church regularly. Aunt Sue and Uncle Bob would never accompany us. In church, I learned there was someone who loved me. His name is Jesus. I held onto that love and prayed to him every day. We also sang in the choir, which I thoroughly enjoyed. I appreciated and cherished my newfound knowledge and love of the Lord. He was always there for me no matter what the circumstances.

Television came into existence about the early '50's. Uncle Bob and Aunt Sue purchased one. Back then this was very big entertainment. This was the era when the popular shows like The Ed Sullivan Show, Arthur Godfrey Hour, Groucho Marx Show, Queen for a Day, The Howdy Doody Show, etc. aired. I was not allowed to watch it. If for some small miracle I was allowed to I had to watch **WITHOUT** my glasses; everything was all fuzzy and blurred. I could hear the T.V. at least.

Once she took us to the movies to see "The Yearling" starring Gregory Peck. She said I was like that little deer, "bad", always getting into trouble and I needed to be punished. She wanted me to learn a lesson from that movie. I couldn't see any connection, because I wasn't mean, never got into trouble, and did not deserve the type of punishment I was dealt. I was never given the chance to misbehave; I just got lashings for doing nothing.

*1 Thessalonians 5:17 "Pray without ceasing."*

# **Chapter 13 "Threats"**

One of my abuser's tactics was to use threats. A common threat was "I dare you to." Living in Chicago we experienced extremely cold nights during the winter months. With snow on the rooftop, our attic room became unbearably cold. Aunt Sue would accommodate me with a heavy green wool army blanket. She'd lay it at the foot of my bed and **"DARE"** me to cover up with it. I would lay there with a thin sheet over me and shiver throughout the night. If I didn't want to be rewarded with a beating, I didn't **DARE** touch that blanket even though I knew how warm I would be with it.

Uncle Sammy also worked for the Baltimore and Ohio Railroad checking boxcars. His hours were from two in the early morning, to ten the next day. He also did not become involved in the torture he witnessed. It was as if he were looking the other way. Later, after I was married, he always remembered my birthday and Christmas with a check. It seemed he was trying to make up for his passiveness all those years. While at home he ate, bathed, and slept. When we got home from school, he was asleep, so we had to be quiet. Aunt Sue awakened him at two in the mornings. This was a good time for her to come upstairs and check to see if I was asleep under that warm blanket. This she did every morning she woke Uncle Sammy. Sometimes I would crawl in bed with Rose, snuggling close to her as she had lots of covers. Whenever I heard Aunt Sue bounding up the stairs, I would quickly jump back into my bed, trembling, hoping she hadn't heard me. One more than one occasion, thinking

I could get away with it, I would cover up with that blanket. The consequence was inevitable; disobedience didn't pay.

While Uncle Sammy slept, Aunt Sue and Uncle Bob were both at work. After arriving home from school, my sister would sneak candy, cookies, and bologna and/or ham for me to eat. Once I ate so much bologna I gorged myself. Never being allowed to have these types of food, I made myself sick. Rose tried to take care of me the best she knew how for a child.

All those years, every Saturday, I was expected to wash my bed sheets. Aunt Sue would throw me a big bar of soap. I had to scrub those sheets between my hands in the bathtub until they were clean enough to suit her. Wet sheets aren't the easiest to handle even for an adult, let alone a small child. Then I had to take them outside in the freezing, bitter cold and hang them out on the clothesline to dry.

Aunt Sue owned a small Pekingese dog that would attack me. I guess the dog thought every time she beat me, **I was hurting her!** The dog did what came naturally trying to protect her, his owner. While Aunt Sue was beating me, I was also being bitten by the dog! Even though the dog was little, the bites stung and hurt. Usually chunks were bitten out of my ankles and lower legs. I still have scars from the gashes. It felt like I was suffocating being attacked from above and below. The dog was conveniently tied to the leg of the table so he could reach me at all times. I was never treated nor taken to receive rabies shots. In fact if I contracted any illnesses, she kept me home and doctored me herself. When I caught the big red measles I had to stay in the attic by myself for about two weeks with the curtains drawn because the light hurt my eyes. Everyone was either at work or at school, so I mostly tended to myself.

I developed several more inner ear infections. Waking up with the room spinning, I would fall out of bed and literally crawl down the stairs. The bathroom, which was at the end of the house next to the kitchen, was my destination. I hoped I wouldn't become too nauseated before arriving there. As I made my way staggering along, hardly able to hold my head up I held onto the walls and furniture. Even during the day I wished I could go back to bed and lay down, but I had to sit in that chair anyway. I was never taken to a doctor.

**Psalms 91:4 "He shall cover thee with his feathers, and under his wings shalt thou trust; his truth shall be thy shield and buckler."**

# Chapter 14 "No Place To Run"

By now I know what you the reader must be asking: why, didn't I run away? Where does a frightened child run? We had no friends to speak of. I did have a few friends at school, but not many. We didn't have any real playmates. There were no homes where we could go to visit and play. We never spent the night with friends or were able to invite friends to our house. Uncle Bob and Aunt Sue never had any company, nor did they have any social life outside of our home. We had no other relatives close by.

One time and one time only, I did try to run away. It was Columbus Day, and school was closed. Because knowing what was in for me at home, I went to school anyway. (I was the only one there.) Walking around the schoolyard, I played on the playground, just enjoying being free for once. But my freedom was not to last. I stayed until I thought it time to go home. Rose was in high school and had naturally told Aunt Sue she had no school that day. I lied, for some reason Aunt Sue let me go. I thought I had outwitted her, But she found out the truth, there was no school that day.

While walking back home, a police car drove up beside me. It seemed I had been reported missing. I begged the nice policemen, not to take me back home, anyplace but there. I knew I would get the beating of my life. They did not seem to hear me or understand my situation; they were only doing their job returning a (presumed) missing child. And yes, I did get the beating of my life. No place to run, no place to hide, no one to help, living every day in fear. When Aunt Sue came at me, I wished I could just disappear. My heart would start racing, and I trembled with fear. I was severely traumatized, physically and mentally and felt, helpless with terror. I was heartsick from the treatment I received.

**Psalms 121:2 "My help cometh from the Lord, which made heaven and earth."**

# <u>Chapter 15 "Holidays"</u>

I received a very pretty little doll, and Uncle Sammy gave me a nice warm red coat. This was the only Christmas, I remember receiving any gifts Aunt Sue did allow me to try the red coat on; But I was never allowed to wear it, nor was I allowed to play with the pretty little doll. I wondered where that pretty warm red coat went? Rose received a dollhouse, a radio, a pretty doll, some clothes and shoes. For future Christmases, I received nothing. It wasn't because they couldn't afford presents; they both had really good jobs for that era. Nor was it because I'd been good or bad. It was because in her own mean way, she was punishing me for being me. She really must have detested me. Naturally, I was very sad, receiving nothing for Christmas.

Aunt Sue always went all out to prepare a feast at Christmas and Thanksgiving. She made the best oyster dressings. The turkeys and hams she baked were always moist. Her hams were always baked with pineapple rings and cherries on top with a brown glazed topping. When she prepared my plate, I received a small portion of whatever she decided she would dish up for me. I never received a second helping, ever. Each year she decorated a big Christmas tree. She did it all alone, never asking anyone else to help. She placed the single strands of tinsel carefully onto each branch. Then she spaced the decorations and each string of lights just so. When completed the tree was beautiful. Then everyone would gather around, passing out presents, to one-another.

Having been sent to bed beforehand, I was always excluded from these activities. I could hear the festivities going on downstairs, and lay in my bed crying. Naturally as any child would do, I anticipated gifts whether I was told I would not receive any; I still hoped I would. After being disappointed many times, I resigned myself to the fact. Consoling myself, I remembered what Christmas is all about. It is not about receiving toys or presents, but receiving Christ into our hearts and celebrating His Birthday. He is the Greatest Gift of ALL.

**Luke 2:11 "For unto you is born this day in the city of David, a Saviour, which is Christ the Lord."**

# <u>Chapter 16 " The Fashion Trend"</u>

I was told repeatedly, that I supposed to have been a boy and that's why my father gave me a boy's name. Aunt Sue informed me my mother and father looked in the Bible to name me. Mother chose a girl's name, Esther. Father chose a boy's name, Joel. I was given them both. Rose couldn't pronounce Joel, so she began to call me Jo'el, pronounced just like No'el. So Jo'el had stayed with me throughout my life. Usually, I wore boy's clothing and boy's shoes. I did look funny and different. Back in the late 40's early 50's, this was not the appropriate fashion it is today. Girls did not wear boys' attire. You can imagine how different I looked dressed in all boys' clothing. I wore high-top boots that laced crisscross up the front of the boot; which came to my knees. My wardrobe consisted of boys' snow suits, boys' small regular under shirts and a pea coat. All the clothes were rather large on me, but they did keep me warm. This remained my wardrobe for all those years.

Rose attended a co-ed high school. She never liked school, so she always skipped classes. She would go off riding with some of her friends. When she was about 15, she began to smoke. I never knew where she went or what she did while she was joyriding with her friends. Wanting to become an artist she found that all the other subjects she was required to take were boring her. When it was time to go home from school, she would always be back from joyriding in plenty of time. After Aunt Sue found out she was skipping school, and smoking, I took the beatings for her punishment. Whenever my sister talked back or cursed Aunt Sue, I took the brunt of her punishments. My sister was slapped some of the times, but I received most of the beatings and punishments for both of us. Rose told me years later she hated Aunt Sue for all the mean things she did to me. Rose couldn't do anything to help me. She must have had an overwhelming feeling of helplessness. Obviously, both of us were too small, we just faced the hardships that were thrown at us the best we could.

Several times I remember being taken to a big building downtown where I was ushered into a very small room. These people asked me to put pieces of puzzles together, to put shapes and blocks into their proper places and slots according to the shapes and sizes. For the life of me, I couldn't do it. Maybe I had a lapse of memory or was trying too hard as these were timed events. I'd stay in that little room for what seemed like hours trying my very best. I never accomplished much. It seems like my Aunt was trying her utmost to have me put away. Back then they put people that were different or slow (retarded) into insane asylums. This way she wouldn't have to deal with me anymore, the state would. After I was grown and married, Uncle Al told my husband about this hateful deed, her trying to have me committed.

**John 14:27 "Let not your heart be troubled, neither let it be afraid."**

# Chapter 17 "Prayer"

Many nights, I would pray to the Lord, to please take me out of this miserable situation, if it was his will, so I could have peace. I wanted to die. My Aunt told me I was the cause of my mother's death. Of course, I didn't know any better at the time. Believing her, I dreamed my mother would appear in my room late at night. I thought I actually could see her; I had a vision of her standing at the foot of my bed. Believing that I had caused my own mother's death, I lived with this horrible guilt. This was another reason why my father didn't want me, I thought. Thus I suffered mental abuse. Unbeknownst to me, the Lord was working on answering my prayers, but it would be years later before his answers were revealed.

Never raising their voices at one another, our Aunt and Uncle appeared to have a good marriage. Although they seemed to get along fine, Uncle Bob couldn't tolerate the abuse any longer. When I was about 11 years old, he filed for divorce. He came to school one day, walking us home, he told us, "goodbye." I imagined he went back home to the farm in Missouri.

Before he left for good, he went to the juvenile authorities to give his account of the abuse going on at our home. Naturally, when they came out to investigate, there again was no evidence of anything out of the ordinary. So, it appeared as if his accusations were false. Not long after the divorce, my Aunt met another man. He moved into the house with us. His name was Richard, a friend of Uncle Sammy's, several years younger than she.

**Isaiah 65:24** "And it shall come to pass, that before they call, I will answer, and while they are yet speaking, I will hear."

# Chapter 18 "High School"

Taking the bus to and from school, I attended Lucy Flower High School for girls. It was a three-story building located in downtown Chicago. My classes were scattered from the first floor to the third. We climbed the stairs, which were very wide and steep, to get from class to class. I had a few friends, but, as in grammar school, not many. Having always liked school, I found high school to be no different. I still made good grades. In school it wasn't easy though, I didn't tell anyone what was happening for fear of another beating for confiding in someone. I just clammed up.

When I became a freshman, I had to dress out for gym, wearing a one-piece big, green bloomer-type gym suit. My legs were visible from the thighs down. I liked taking gym; it gave me freedom from sitting. As I was too short to play, my gym teacher, Mrs., McCutheon, chose me to referee the Volleyball games. I enjoyed all my classes, but gym was my favorite class of all. During gym, Mrs. McCutheon began to notice the bruises on my legs, and began questioning me. I did not want to tell her for fear, first of all, that no one would actually believe me and secondly I didn't want another beating for telling. So, I told her I just ran into a door. Of course she didn't buy that!!

Mrs. McCutheon then sent me to the school's Counselor, Mrs. Schaefer. Mrs. Schaefer urged me to tell her the truth. She said it wasn't possible that I kept running into doors, every day causing me to come to school with bruises all over my legs all the time, especially bruises that looked like that. The bruises were from the beatings with the 2x4. So, day after day, week after week, I sat with Mrs. Schaefer in her office because she said I couldn't go back to any of my classes until I told her how and where I received those bruises. Well, I did want to keep my grades up. Knowing I wasn't doing myself any good just sitting day after day, with my school work not getting done, I thought what have I got to lose? Finally it all came tumbling out, all the ugly details of this horrible nightmare that was happening to me. To my surprise, she was the first person to believe me. I was amazed to say the least! But this was her job she was a school counselor. And too, the whelps on the fronts and backs of my thighs and legs were evidence SOMETHING was happening other than me running into the door.

**Hebrew 13:6 "So that we may boldly say, The Lord is my helper, and I will not fear what man shall do unto me."**

# Chapter 19 "Juvenile Authorities"

Mrs. Schaefer advised me to go to the juvenile authorities. Assuring me they would be able to help, she set up the appointment for me. One day after school my sister and I rode the "L" train to uptown Chicago to keep the appointment while Aunt Sue was at work. A nice little gray-haired lady, Mrs. Creighton came over and asked if she could help us. As I handed her Mrs. Schaefer's note, she said she'd been waiting for us. Filled with anticipation, I began spilling out my anguish, pouring out my heart and soul about this mad woman whom I felt was at the time trying to kill me little by little. After reliving all the nightmarish details, to my horror she didn't believe me. She said, and her exact words were, "Little girl, go home, no one could be that cruel to anyone, let alone a child. You are just making all of this up." Things like that did not happen in our grand society. Working with abused children was her specialty, but yet she didn't believe me!!

How could I have imagined this harrowing, incredibly, horrible nightmare? I actually was living this "make believe" nightmare that was consuming so much of my life. I wondered how could I get it across to her so she would listen and understand the anguish I was feeling. Being very pessimistic, she said that I wanted to get attention and making up the horrible fairy tale was my way of getting it. Needless to say, I cried; I felt betrayed. As we were leaving her office I vowed never to put my trust in another adult again!

As fate would have it, when Uncle Bob had gone to the juvenile authorities, it just so happened he had spoken to the same lady I had been talking with, Mrs. Creighton!! The Lord was working here and had been for all those years on my behalf. After we left, that evening Mrs. Creighton went home and couldn't, get me off her mind. It came to her that seemingly five years before a grown man had come to her with the same awful, incredible story. The next day upon arriving at work, she began digging in her file cabinet for my file. She found it in the basement (at the time they kept only current files upstairs.) All files five years old or older were stored in the basement. She began reading from my uncle's five-year-old report almost word for word what I had conveyed to her the day before. She immediately called Mrs. Schaefer and instructed her to inform me to return to her office. I had no intentions of returning, but Mrs. Schaefer relayed to me of Mrs. Creighton's findings, of my uncle going to her five years before, so my fictitious fairy tale was incredibly true. (Dear Lord, Thank You, for answering my prayers.)

During this time a cousin on my father's side, John, was stationed with the Army in Chicago. Our Father asked him to look us up. John came to the door one day (our Aunt was at work), and asked about us. Uncle Sammy was outside painting the house he let John in. At first we didn't know him, he was all grown up and married. The last time we'd seen him, he was a young boy. He was shocked at the appearance of the house. With everything looking so drab and dreary he questioned why were we living in what appeared to him to be a morgue like atmosphere? We quickly told him all that had been taking place in our lives all throughout the years. John was appalled and said he would call our father, explain the situation to him, and see if he would want us back. John knew our father had no knowledge of all that had been taking place in our young

47

lives. He had a different view of happiness and love, which was what he had been reading from the letters our aunt, had sent him. John left with the promise he would get in touch with our father and we would be hearing back from him.

**Psalms 33:21 "For our heart shall rejoice in him, because we have trusted in his holy name."**

# Chapter 20 "Escape"

In the meantime Rose was preparing to leave home. On her next birthday she would be 18 years old, and at 18 you could be on your own. She packed a suitcase, sneaked it down the stairs, and carried it to the corner grocery store. Mrs. Ethridge, the storeowner allowed us to leave it at her store. Rose also sent off for our birth certificates, (which were to be mailed to the store), as she felt we would need them if she was to apply for a job, and I was to continue to attend school. She really didn't have any idea of where she was going, but she knew she had to leave and take me with her. It was as though my cousin's visit was a sign from the Lord. When John notified our father, he was ready to come get us, but it would be two weeks before he could get a train to arrive.

John and his wife Grace were renting a small apartment, we picked up the suitcase, following John's instructions, and we took a cab, and stayed with them for a while. Aunt Sue was all upset, calling the police and reporting us as runaways. To this day, Rose was afraid she would be arrested for kidnapping; although this was not what took place, but these were her feelings. If I had been left there this would have been the ruination of me, I would have been history. I know I wouldn't have been on this earth much longer; as angry as Aunt Sue was when the juvenile authorities notified her of my coming to them for help.

We were again summoned back to the Juvenile Hall. Mrs. Creighton advised me I would need witnesses to help my case. Rose and Uncle Sammy had to testify in my behalf when we appeared in court. The Juvenile Hall notified my natural father of all that had taken place and also to see if he would be willing to take me back to live with him. Mrs. Creighton did not send me back home to Aunt Sue. She held me in Protective Custody and placed me in the Juvenile Detention Hall. Here I stayed until the court date. This was a very scary place, but no one bothered me. I remember I had to undress, as I had to take a shower. I was given a gown of some sort to wear, then placed in a room by myself. I didn't know about the different kinds of girls there were, I was so naïve. They did laugh and made fun of me, but that was the least of my worries, I had endured much worse than that. Father arrived two weeks later on the train. Rose said it was a slow cow train, that's why it took him so long to come.

When the court date arrived, I was escorted from the Detention hall straight to the courtroom for the proceedings. The Judge hearing the charges was very angry with my aunt asking her why had she put me through all what I had endured. Aunt Sue's ludicrous explanation to him was that she NEVER wanted me to begin with. She despised me, only wanting my sister because she said; Rose was the apple of her eye. After the final decision, the judge awarded me back to my father; he shouted at my aunt; for everyone to hear: "If I had known before hand what I just witnessed, I would have taken you by the hair of your head and mopped up this courtroom floor with you." What happened to Aunt Sue? NOTHING absolutely NOTHING!! As far as the court system goes, nothing was done to her. She showed no remorse what so ever for all the horrifying years she had put my sister and me through. But as she was leaving on the bus going back home, she looked so depressed and defeated.

On the way out of the courtroom that day my Aunt informed me, "Well, now see what you've done to yourself.

50

You have a criminal record. You've been locked up, and that will stay with you the rest of your life!!" She spoke as though I was a hardened criminal!! I was only held in Protective Custody for protection from HER!! Her boy friend, Richard, who was living in the house with us, helped my case also. The judge acknowledged this was no environment for two teen-aged girls. After we moved, Aunt Sue and Richard married. The Judge asked our father if he wanted our name changed back to his. Since we were girls, he said no, because eventually when we married our names would change anyway. We were blessed to be finally free. Sometimes the system waits until a child is dead before they step in. Then it is too late. Unfortunately the system fails so many children.

**Matthew 19:26 "But with God all things are possible."**

# Chapter 21 "Back to Louisiana"

Riding the train back to New Orleans was really interesting and enjoyable. It had been eight long years since we had really seen our father, he seemed like a stranger to us. He began to teach us how to cook, clean, wash dishes, and buy groceries. These were the things we didn't learn to do with my aunt; we had never been in a grocery store with her. Our father took us shopping, buying us as many new clothes as possible. He was trying his best to make up for all those lost years. Now we were teenagers and could be left in the house while he still worked the midnight shift. We became re-acquainted with our cousins, going to the movies, riding the streetcars, enjoying Mardi Gras parades and festivals. This was more freedom than we had ever had; in so long a time; it was like another world had opened up for us. My cousin, Anna, and I attended church regularly. At the age of 17, I accepted the Lord Jesus Christ into my life experiencing so much joy and happiness. Warmth I had never known entered my WHOLE BEING as I received my Lord into my heart. I was totally filled with His Love.

When we moved back to New Orleans, in 1954; I was 16 years old and weighed all of 60 pounds! I looked like a scarecrow, with toothpick arms and legs. Even though, I have many good memories of this time. Several of our relatives got together the next spring, give me a SURPRISE Birthday Party (my first). I was 17 years old!! I can't remember all the gifts if received except one. My father gave me a little parakeet. He was so pretty, with different shades of blue and a yellow breast. I named him Jimmy!

After settling back in with our father, I enrolled into Sacred Heart Catholic High School. I rode the Canal Street car there, as it was located right on Canal Street. The girls wore uniforms of white blouses and blue skirts. The boys wore uniforms of khaki shirts and pants. I was very happy during my last year and a half. My grades were fairly good. I joined several activities, something I wasn't allowed to before. We marched before each football game, twirling big flags, marching in step to the sounds of the band; we were the marching flag corp. During my junior year, I was elected class secretary and enjoyed playing volleyball. I also served as part-time librarian and helped in the school office.

School dances were held every Friday night for the student body. I never learned to dance, and never had any dates, but I joined in anyway. Dancing with some of my girlfriends' boyfriends', I learned to dance the jitterbug, and the twist; these were popular dances back in the late '50's. We danced to the music of Fats Domino, Elvis Presley, Dion and the Bell Hops, Bobby Darren, Bill Haley and the Comets. Other artists were Bobby Riddle, Chubby Checker, Dee Dee Sharp, Percy Sledge and the Drifters; too many more to mention. Some of the popular songs then were entitled: "Sixteen Candles," "I'll Cry if I Want To", "Teen Angel", "Lolly Pop, Lolly Pop", "Purple People Eater", "Chantilly Lace", "Crying in the Chapel", "Rock Around the Clock", "Walking to New Orleans", "Blue Suede Shoes", "Jail House Rock", "The Great Pretender", "Can't Help Falling In Love", "Hound Dog", "In the Ghetto", "Unchained Melody", "Blue Berry Hill", "Only You", and "Roses are Red"; among others.

Because she had not graduated yet, Rose enrolled in a co-ed public school, Warren Eastern that was right across

53

the street from Sacred Heart. In 1956 just a few months before I graduated, she graduated. When I graduated a few of my relatives, Aunt Kit, father and Rose came. Afterward father took us out to eat at the Blue Room. This was very special for us.

Rose was employed at a department store in downtown New Orleans. One of her co-workers introduced Rose to her brother. They dated and soon were married in December of 1956. She married 2 months before I did. Seems the love-bug bit us both about the same time. This was only about two years after we came back to live with our father. Our lives had changed so much during that time. Father became upset at the idea of us getting married. It seems he had just become acquainted with his girls. Rose and her husband settled in New Orleans so at least one of us was close by.

**Habakkuk 3:18 "Yet I will rejoice in the Lord, I will joy in the God of my salvation."**

# Chapter 22 "DeWitt"

After graduating from high school in the spring of 1956, I met a very nice young man. His name was DeWitt. I was employed part-time after school and on weekends at a local hospital. I worked at the information desk, admitting, and relieving at the switchboard. By now I was working full time. DeWitt worked at the same hospital in Central Supply. I had been praying to the Lord if it were to be Your will, to send me someone to love. I really didn't think he would, especially that soon, but he did. He sent DeWitt to me.

The very fist time DeWitt ever saw me, I had previously picked a pimple causing blood poisoning with a red streak going up the side of my face. My face was all swollen and I was wearing a scarf to hide the hideous bruise the pimple had made. As I was making my way to the emergency room for treatment DeWitt saw me briefly in passing. Later, he conveyed how sorry he felt for me and how cute he thought I was!

DeWitt began asking one of our fellow workers Glenn, to ask me out. Glenn came to me and asked me to ask Jackie to go out with him! Jackie worked as a secretary in Medical Records. We began to double date. On our dates we rode around Lake Ponchartrain, or went to drive in movies. Many nights, we would just drive to Lake Ponchartrain, and watch the lights of the boats as they sailed by. Jackie and Glenn are still very dear, close friends after all these years. At present they reside in Mississippi and have four children and several grandchildren.

When I first met DeWitt, I didn't care for him. As I was extremely shy, maybe I was too scared of my own feelings. All the old sayings, which had been drilled into my head, kept haunting me. I almost sent him on his way. After two weeks of dating, he told me he loved me! Now I could hardly believe him. Not knowing quite how to react to all this attention, I asked him how could he know he loved me, as he hardly knew me. But, he professed his love for me anyway. Here was someone other than my Lord and my sister who loved me. After dating nine months, we became engaged and were married on February 23$^{rd}$, 1957. He was my first date, my one and only love.

Our wedding was small and simply beautiful. Most of our friends from the hospital and our immediate family attended. DeWitt's suit cost all of $7.00; it was a pretty nice light powder blue. My wedding gown, which I borrowed from one of my cousins', was soft white full-skirted, trimmed with a lot of lace and netting. Our reception was held at another cousin's home. It all seemed like a fairy tale come true. We honeymooned in Biloxi, Mississippi. We hardly noticed it rained the whole weekend we were gone. Our first home was an 8' x 28' mobile travel trailer. Even though it was small, it was ours, and to me it was a mansion.

DeWitt was a very wonderful husband, loving and kind. I'm not saying we didn't have our ups and downs; what marriage doesn't? But, most of our married life was happy. He loved to pick at me, always giving me different nicknames. For example, he'd call me "Mozelle", instead of Jo'el. He was a very hard worker. From the time he was three years old, when he wasn't asleep or eating, he was working. He was an outdoorsman, loved to work on the farm, or in the woods. Working very hard to give us a good life, he provided well for his little family. He loved his children and grandchildren more than anything. He just loved children in general; he had a very big heart. He also loved horses and cows; we had several horses and a herd of dairy cows on our farm.

**Matthew 21:22 "And all things, whatsoever ye shall ask in prayer, believing, ye shall receive."**

# Chapter 23 "Hurricane Audrey"

My husband and his family own an 80-acre dairy farm in Southwest Louisiana. DeWitt or his father picked up the milk from the surrounding dairies in the area (about a 200-mile radius). They hauled the milk by truck to the Borden Milk Plant in Lake Charles, La. At first the milk was picked up in milk cans and kept cold with big blocks of square ice, as there were no refrigerated trucks back then. The milk was picked up 365 days a year and the farm was run 365 days a year.

Before we completely moved to the country, we came for a short visit during June 1957. His mother and father took a vacation to visit their other children in different parts of Texas. While they were gone, we encountered "Hurricane Audrey". This was our first experience with such a devastating storm of this nature. I was six months pregnant with our first child. Unaware that the storm had become a hurricane, DeWitt and Leland, our neighbor boy, and a very good friend, left to run the milk route. It began to rain in squalls early that morning with lightening flashing and thunder crashing terribly, and not letting up.

I was left in the house alone, with no lights, no phones, no windows, and no way of knowing this was a hurricane. The windows all blew out. Water was coming in from all sides of the house and the doors swung opened. The more I'd try to wipe up the rainwater, the more the wind blew it back in. So finally I just left it. I was fighting a losing battle. Then I was thinking DeWitt would turn around and come back home, but the milk must be hauled, just like the mail must go through. One of our neighbors, Mr. Fogelman, came to my rescue. Before he took me to his house I wrote a note to DeWitt telling him where I would be, but the wind and rain blew it away, he never found that note. Mr. Fogelman's son, Buddy, went out in the storm looking for DeWitt to let him know were I was. He had a terrible time finding the milk truck, but having some knowledge of the milk route that DeWitt took (sometimes he joined DeWitt on the route) he finally was able to locate him. When the storm hit it blew down a big mulberry tree on top of the roof of the house where I'd been taken for shelter. All around us there was flooding, and damage to almost every house and structure.

DeWitt and Leland, unaware of the storm, kept on picking up the dairymen's milk until one of them, Mr. Silas McKee, ran out to the barn and informed them of the hurricane they were in. They had been thinking that the weather was bad and it wouldn't last long. The further they drove, they came upon fallen trees and had to get out in the pouring rain drag the uprooted trees out of their path so they could continue on the route.

This particular storm hit Cameron, Louisiana, doing devastating damage to the coastline. It also did severe and heavy damage to other surrounding towns, Cameron, Louisiana included. The next day we went to the port of Lake Charles to help with the evacuation. There were so many people coming in by boats that had either lost loved ones or seen them swept away. One young girl in particular kept crying out, "I can't find my mother and father. My name is Audrey. This is why they are lost, because the storm was named after me." We tried to comfort her, assuring her this was not why her folks were lost. We prayed all the lost would be found. If I remember correctly

59

there were approximately five hundred people killed in Hurricane Audrey.

Audrey was not the only storm I have endured. Over the years we have encountered many more hurricanes, including Hurricane Camille. Also several tornadoes have touched down in our neck of the woods. Three have taken the extending roof off of my mobile home, in which I now live. Tornadoes are very scary, and they do sound just like a freight train coming at you!! I can vouch for that; I've been in this mobile home twice out of the three times the tornadoes have hit. People comment, saying I must live in Tornado Alley. The Lord has heard my prayers and has spared my mobile home and me.

**Psalms 120:1 "In my distress, I cried unto the Lord, and he heard me."**

# Chapter 24 "New Life"

In June of 1958, we moved to the farm, which is located on the outskirts of the quaint little town of DeRidder, a parish seat of a dry parish in southwest Louisiana. One of the tourist attractions, in this little town is the Hanging Jail. Built in 1914, it has the Collegiate Gothic design. DeRidder also has the first USO (United Service Organization), building in the nation. It was built in 1941; the service men stationed at Fort Polk, Louisiana came here for recreation. One annual attraction is a Doll Festival, which features over 3000 dolls.

DeWitt and his family were the turning point, a big influence, in my newfound life. They showered me with love I never knew existed. There were many adjustments for this city girl though. We had no indoor bathroom, only an outhouse!! There was no way of taking a bath except by washbasin, and drawing water. This was the biggest adjustment for me, having lived most of my life in large cities.

My father was most upset with me because after I married, I moved away. Although my present living conditions were not what he would have had in mind for me. In the country there is always lots of fresh air, I could see stars clearly for miles! The house we moved into had no screens on the windows. Whenever I'd open a window, the cows would just poke their heads in for a short visit. We also had no telephone, each farm was miles apart. On my father's first visit here, he surveyed my surroundings. Knowing we had no indoor bathroom, he was more than ready for me to return with him to the city. He didn't think I

61

would ever adjust. But adjust I did; I was here to stay. He came quite often throughout the years for visits; helping us plant our gardens, and tending to the chickens. He didn't care too much about helping us milk the cows, though! When he'd return to New Orleans, he'd plant a small garden for himself, my sister and her family.

We raised chickens, pigs, sheep, and had a few horses. Also we milked 80 Holstein cows and ran the milk route. At that time we were still hauling in milk cans. Years later, we were the first milk haulers' from Louisiana to purchase a 5600 gallon refrigerated, all stain-less steel milk tank. We drove to Fond de Lac, Wisconsin to purchase it.

Our little family was raised on this farm. We had two precious, beautiful children, a girl and a boy. After my eldest daughter was born, I'd sit for hours just holding her looking and marveling at the miracle of her. Here was this little creature for me to love and cherish, and she was mine. I prayed to the Lord to please bless us with a healthy baby. He did; she was perfect. When we lost our little boy, Aunt Sue's awful words kept ringing in my head: "If you have children, they won't live!" He died of infectious encephalitis when he was only three months old. Why would any human being tell another human such horrible things? She was an insidious monster and a maniac. We grieved for him so. After a year of grieving a neighbor lady bought a book written by Dale Evans Rogers entitled "Angels Unaware", for me. Reading it helped. We know he has gone on to start our family circle in Heaven.

After several miscarriages, we finally were able to adopt a precious son and precious daughter, making our little family complete. This was a very rewarding experience. We waited for our little son for 11 months before he was placed with us. For our little daughter, we waited 8 months. The joy we experienced, when the calls came to pick them up was only equaled by the joy of the births of our two other children. Not everyone's reaction to this situation was the same. My aunt Sue adopted us, and she did not appreciate the gift of child. DeWitt and I having had children of our own were fortunate to have adopted children. We thanked the Lord everyday for these wonderful blessings our children.

Rose and her husband Raymond raised five children, two boys and three girls. When her oldest son was 17, he was shot and killed standing on their front porch. She often remarked how odd it was that both of our eldest sons had died. It almost seemed like Aunt Sue had put a curse on us.

After this terrible tragedy, while getting their lives back together Rose and her family came and lived with us for a short time. Our father also lived with us for a short period of time. Then, they all moved back to New Orleans. This is where Rose lives today near her children. Father never remarried, he passed away several years after moving back home.

Uncle Carlo and his wife, Eva, came to visit us. They thoroughly enjoyed the fresh country air and the wide-open spaces. Marveling at all the stars, they stayed a week with us. During the years several of my second cousins from New Orleans came to visit. Everyone know how city folk love to visit their country cousins!

Jerry and Bobby, two of my second cousins, came every summer just as soon as school was out. They were eight and ten years old when they first started coming. Either their folks brought them, or they came by Greyhound bus. Every year, a few weeks before school let out, they were packing their bags. They were going to the country! These two boys helped DeWitt with the milking, hauling the hay, riding and helping him on the milk route. They worked hard, loved coming and staying the summers with us. We loved having them; they felt towards DeWitt as their second father. Even though they were from the city, they handled their fair share of the workload on the farm. As they were a tremendous help to us, these years were not wasted. It was learning and growing experience for them both.

Several of our customers on the milk route thought Jerry was my little brother, as he favored me. Not having any brother, this was a nice compliment. They came for about ten years or more, until they each were of college age. DeWitt had pet names for them; he christened Jerry, "Clyde" and Bobby "R.J." He had nicknames for most all of the children in our lives. Several more of my cousins and also several nieces and nephews came off and on to visit. It was like we had summer camp on the farm. We enjoyed each and every one of them throughout the years. DeWitt and I always had a houseful of children and company by the dozens.

For recreation, our family joined Riding Club, and event for the entire family. It is fashioned after the big rodeos, except held locally. Each family member from young to adult participates in any event they chose. The events consisted of Riding Barrels, Bare Back Riding, Calf Roping, etc. Our little family won many, many trophies.

**1 Thessalonians 5:18 "In every thing give thanks."**

# Chapter 25 "Mama and Daddy"

I learned how to trust, to love and be loved and to become socially acceptable. I felt like a new person, the Lord had given me a second chance at life. During this time I tried to put the past behind me and enjoy my future. This was a time to come out of my shell, to live, laugh and enjoy life to the fullest. My in-laws were Mennonite Christian people. Before I married, I knew nothing of the Mennonite Faith, but since have come to love these people dearly. They are very hard working, honest people who live the Bible in their everyday lives and show their love for their fellow man. As I had not really known a mother or father during those years of abuse, I loved them like they were my real parents. I always called them Mama and Daddy. They were the most wonderful mother-in-law and father-in-law a person could have wished for. We all worked side by side every day on the farm. Our lives were intertwined with one another.

My in-laws came to Southwest Louisiana from Southeast Texas in the late 40's. They had purchased an eighty-acre tract of land for about $4.00 an acre. To pay for the land, they dug out and hauled pin knots to the tall oil or turpentine plant. This was backbreaking work. There was a small chicken house on the land; this is where they lived until they were able to build a small house. They acquired several milk cows, milking them by hand at a neighbor's dairy barn. Later, they were in the position to purchase more cows, and stared their own dairy.

My father-in-law was previously in the Calvary in his younger years. While in the Calvary his task was shoeing horses. When they arrived here on the farm, he was the only farrier for miles around. Watching him as he made horseshoes was an education in itself. First he built a big fire in the forge, and then he blew it with a bellow until the heat increased to the right temperature. You could hear the loud pinging as he swung his hammer down on the horseshoes, which he positioned on top of his anvil. Sparks would fly as he shaped that shoe, turning it until he shaped it to the right fit for the horses' hoof. This was very hard work, but he loved making and fitting horseshoes. He also drove an eighteen-wheeler milk truck, picking up the 10-gallon cans of milk from the surrounding dairies for many years. When he no longer could drive the trucks, his youngest son who started to drive at thirteen took over. This young man became my future husband.

My mother-in-law worked all of her life; in fact, this was a family of hard workers. They took me in like I was one of their own. Mama would start her mornings about 3:00 a.m. She'd herd the cows into the milk barn, place them into their milk stalls, pour up their feed and put the milkers on them. Back then we didn't have modern electric milkers which allowed the milk to go straight from the cow into the glass tubes and run down into the stainless milk tank. The milk went from the milkers into a stainless steel can, and then Mama would have to pour this into the 10-gallon cans.

Mama then would lift up the 10-gallon milk cans with the help of her knee and place them down into the milk cooler. She was the one who actually taught me how to cook, all that I learned I learned from her. She taught me very useful lessons on kindness, patience, love and how to work. I couldn't keep up with her. She was always outdoing herself. She also raised leghorn chickens. This was a job in itself. During the years she also fixed and mended the fences, plowed and planted the fields for hay, raised rows of cotton, which she picked. She'd plow, plant and dig sweet potatoes and also planted and picked Louisiana red-hot Tabasco peppers. She also quilted beautifully, along with all the other chores of keeping house, cooking and washing on a wringer washing machine. Years later she opened a Bake Shop in our small town, besides baking pies, cakes and breads, she made the best doughnuts that melted in your mouth.

I felt like Ruth from the Old Testament. DeWitt's people became my people. Their way of life became mine. I had yearned for a mother all those years, and she became that mother. This whole family was very precious to me. I loved DeWitt, my mother-in-law and my father-in-law very much. There are not enough words to express how much I loved them. There was no comparison between this life style and the one I had previously lived. This was a very loving family. I learned how to drive on the farm on the backcountry roads; first driving the tractors, then a car, and then a pick-up truck. These all had standard transmissions. Helping my husband with the milk route I also learned to drive our eighteen-wheeler. This was a wonderful life. Even though there was always a lot of work to be done, we took time for family fun. When finished with chores, we fished and camped out by our pond, building a campfire to roast hot dogs and marshmallows. Then we slept under the stars wrapped in blankets. We walked in the woods, enjoying all of God's marvelous works of nature, the landscape and the wild animals. We've encountered deer, squirrels, coyotes, fox, wild hogs, bobcats, skunks, snakes, red cardinals, blue jays, mallard ducks, owls, road-runners, chicken hawks, various species of birds, even a black bear in the woods near our farm.

Don't get me wrong. On the farm we worked 365 days a year. If we weren't picking up pine knots, we picked cotton. We also picked Louisiana hot peppers, milked the cows every day, cut, raked, baled and hauled our own hay. There was never a dull moment on the farm. Mama taught me how to sew, quilt, and put up vegetables from our garden by canning and freezing them. Also I learned to make homemade jellies and to bake bread. Making lots of handicrafts for my family, I taught myself how to crochet and knit.

**Ruth 1:16 "For whither thou goest, I will go; and where thou lodgest, I will lodge; thy people shall be my people; and thy God my God."**

# Chapter 26 "Aunt Sue and Uncle Kato"

Some year's later Aunt Sue's second husband, Richard, divorced her too. One day out of the blue, she called wanting to come live near us here in the country. Explaining she didn't want to live in the city any longer. Why she decided this, I'm not quite sure, but my kind husband invited her to do so rent-free. He pulled her trailer to a nice shady spot on our farm. DeWitt and his family had never known such horrible people existed. It was very hard to convince him and all of his family of the mean and cruel things she had done. His was a very happy and loving childhood. I had my doubts, and the ole' real fear was there again.

I never did trust her. She had always said, "A leopard never changes its spots". I wondered could she change hers. After she lived here awhile, she asked me to leave my eldest child with her, but I couldn't not for a minute, without me being there. She also began to attend church with us. All who became acquainted with her liked her. They would say, "Is this the aunt that took you in and gave you a home?" She seemed so nice and sweet she won over my husband and his entire family. Little did they know!

My husband's Uncle Kato came for a visit. He and Aunt Sue became friends. Ironically, they became such good friends they married! Her multiple personality, the kind and gentle self was at work here befriending a lot of our kin on my husband's side. They couldn't see how someone as sweet and nice as she appeared could have done all what I accused her of.

She and Uncle Kata moved to Arizona to live near my eldest sister-in-law Maud and her young son, Grant. Aunt Sue began taking care of Grant while Maud worked. At first Aunt Sue was sweet and kind to Grant. **BUT**, the mean and hateful side of her was surfacing again. She began to hide food from Grant (special foods his mother had bought especially for him) and was cruel to him, not physically, but mentally. She would eat the food his mother had left for him and give him whatever foods she didn't want.

Maud could not stand for this, and it was becoming quite clear to her that all the things I had accused Aunt Sue of were true. Maud wrote a letter to me, apologizing to me in particular for not having believed me throughout the years. Aunt Sue also began to become physically abusive toward Uncle Kato. She began to beat him over the head with her high-heel shoes just as she had done to me. She even went as far as to take his own shotgun to him. This brought the police to their residence.

After several years passed by, Uncle Kata died, and we attended his funeral. Aunt Sue kept repeating, I was the only member of her family there she kept clinging to me. She was my aunt and her husband, Uncle Kata, was my husband's Uncle.

**James 4:10 "Humble yourselves in the sight of the Lord, and he shall lift you up."**

# Chapter 27 "Cancer"

I was 33 years old when I was diagnosed with cancer. My first thoughts were I am the same age as mother when she died. In 1970 the word cancer was like a death sentence, the doctors were not as up to date on how to treat many types of cancer. The word cancer is still like a death sentence but more cures and more knowledge are available today than they were back then. Cigarette smoke was not known to be harmful to your health especially second hand-smoke. I never smoked or drank, but I was exposed to second-hand smoke over the years and had severe headaches frequently. To find the cause we went to several clinics, even the Diagnostic Clinic in Houston. After being seen by an allergist we were told I was highly allergic to cigarette smoke, among other things. Back then it hadn't been proven that anyone could become allergic to cigarette smoke. I was one of the first. Naturally no one believed this to be possible.

The doctor told DeWitt he needed to quit smoking for his sake as well as the children's and mine. He informed the doctor if it had been one of our children he probably would try to quit. Years later he finally began to smoke outside the house, but the damage had been done to us both. I had cervical cancer, and eighteen years later DeWitt developed lung cancer. I received twenty cobalt treatments in a span of about four months. They cause me to become so nauseated that I lost weight and slept most of the time. Each treatment I took was in an enclosed room where I had to go alone, but the Lord was with me all the way. I would pray the Lord's Prayer each and every time I lay there under that huge machine that blasted the radiation into me. Then, the doctors implanted the raw radiation into me for seventy-two hours. This literally burned me inside and out.

At the same time while I was in the hospital, our eldest daughter, Therese, had broken her knee in a motorcycle accident and had to have surgery. We were in different hospitals approximately 65 miles apart. In order to visit us both, DeWitt had to drive all that way to visit me and all that way to see Therese. I was unable to see her until I came home. With out the help from Evelyn one of my sisters-in-law, and her small daughter, Kaye, our wonderful Mennonite neighbors, especially Margie Schmidt and her family, plus my in-laws, I would not have made it. As the children were quite small they came and helped with my family, cooking, cleaning and tending to me as well. The Lord healed me. I've been cancer free for 29 years now.

**Psalms 23:4 "Yea, though I walk through the valley of the shadow of death, I will fear no evil; for thou art with me; thy rod and thy staff they comfort me."**

# Chapter 28 "No Longer Farmers"

My husband decided that he wanted to plant soybeans; along with everything else we had on the farm. But, when the price to sell went down, the bottom fell out. We were forced out and off the land. I used to sit and cry watching all the farmers up north in Iowa and places like that being forced out and off their land. Three years later when it happened to us, I was very angry, I didn't shed the first tear. Farmers work so hard and then the bank or the lien holder can just come and take everything away. I held down three jobs hoping this would help with expenses; but all was in vain. After 28 ½ years of marriage we were moved off the farm. Our equipment, the cows, barn and house and land were all sold. All we had left was our personal possessions, our clothes, household goods, and furniture. We no longer had a vehicle it was also taken. We started all over again. This was hard, but was even harder on the children.

Our children were not used to living in a 12.80 mobile home, without central heat and air and with no insulation. We had been living in a four-bedroom brick home that did have central heat and air; now we had a few acres and a mobile home. Having only one ceiling fan, we burned up in the summer and in the winter we chopped wood for our small wood heater that sat in the living room. In the bedrooms and bathroom we either froze or burned up. Long before this time: DeWitt and I had lived this way; but the children had not. It was as if we were going backwards instead of forward, but at least we were thankful we had someplace to live. A lot of farmers who also were forced out didn't have anything, no land, no house, nothing. We were extremely grateful for what little we did have, and learned to adjust.

Since our bread and butter no longer came from the land, we both were lucky to find work. I started an answering service here at home, running it twenty-four hours a day, seven days a week for seven years. DeWitt became employed in town working for a construction company. After the construction job played out, he began driving an eighteen-wheeler again; hauling timber (long wood) to the Boise Paper Mill on the other side of town. Not long after all of this, things began to really take a turn for the worse.

**Hebrews 13:5 "And be content with such things as ye have: for he hath said, I will never leave thee, nor forsake thee."**

# Chapter 29 "Gone, But Not Forgotten"

My father-in-law, getting up in years, began to slow down. He became quite ill, and was bedridden for several years. While still at home one evening just before dark he quietly passed away in November of 1987. He had this peaceful look on his face, and just before he passed he had asked Mama if she saw that beautiful light. He pointed upwards, asked her for a glass of water or ice. When she returned with the glass, he slipped away. The knowledge that he was a very devoted Christian and believed in our Lord and Saviour, made his passing easier to bear. Shortly after, my mother-in-law was diagnosed with skin cancer. A few months later my beloved husband was also diagnosed with lung cancer. This was all such terrible news for our whole family. Neither one had ever been sick, so this was a horrible ordeal for them both.

The Doctor explained to Mama that the kind of cancer she had was caused by the rays of the sun. Whenever she worked outside, she would wear one of Daddy's long sleeve shirts, never taking it off from daylight until dark. She explained that when the wind blew, it made her cooler, so she kept that sweaty shirt on. From the sun beaming down on that shirt, and the seat going down into her skin, caused her to develop this type of skin cancer. She suffered through a few bouts of chemotherapy. The treatments made her so very ill she refused to take any more. Praying the Lord to help her, she slipped away the following year, in March of 1988. She and Daddy had been married for over 67 years. One is never prepared for times like these. It was hard enough to loose Daddy, but so soon after him, Mama! We have the assurance they both have gone to their reward and are with our Lord and Saviour.

After being diagnosed with cancer of the lung, DeWitt threw those cigarettes down and never smoked again. He was smoking three and a half packs a day, and had started to smoke at the age of 15. He told me how sorry he was for having put me through all those years of headaches. Now since he had quite smoking he couldn't stand the smell of cigarettes either. He also had to take chemotherapy and radiation treatments. The treatments caused him to be nauseated, he had never been this sick before. I am thankful I had my business at home, as I could see to Mama, Daddy and take care of DeWitt. He wanted to continue to do as much as he could while he could. Always an outside person, he never could sit idle. A neighbor needed his hay bailed; DeWitt undertook the job, baling the hay just two weeks before he passed away even though he was so ill. After both of his parents passed on, he just gave up. He missed them so very much. Three months after Mama passed away, DeWitt passed away, in July 1988. We had been married for 31 years and six months. Just watching him fight made me believe he would eventually get well. When he didn't, I was devastated. There are not enough words to describe the sorrow that overwhelmed me. I couldn't believe we had lost all three of them in so short a span of time. I yearn to join all of them someday in heaven.

I didn't have time to grieve for Daddy when I was grieving for Mama and then DeWitt. I grieved for them all at once instead of separately. We were all part of each other, seeing and being with one another every day. I still miss them terribly. Being very sad, I did not care to live. Whenever I went outside, I didn't even want the flowers to bloom. Becoming very despondent, I refused to eat because

I didn't want to eat alone. I really leaned on the Lord for comfort and prayed He would give me the strength to continue on. I could have easily gone out of my mind, but He helped me keep my sanity. The Lord and my children, especially my grandchildren came to my rescue. Knowing I had to live gave me the courage to go on. I knew my family still needed me. Over the years several nieces, nephews, and Uncle Sammy, and a precious little infant granddaughter also have passed away. It is very hard to lose loved ones. But, the assurance we will all meet again is a comfort and a blessing.

**"Matthew5:4 "Blessed are they that mourn; for they shall be comforted."**

# Chapter 30 "The Funeral"

When the movie Mommy Dearest and the book by Christina Crawford came out about her mother Joan Crawford, I first read the book, I identified with a lot of the tortures she experienced from living with her cruel mother. Then, I saw the movie. While watching it I began to sink down in the seat as if the scenes on the screen were actually taking place and happening to me. My heart was racing; I was actually feeling the blows and the hateful words. The old fear was back again.

After I received the call that Aunt Sue had passed away (she lived to be 89 years old), I knew I had to attend that funeral. As I stood beside her coffin looking upon her, I had mixed emotions: with tears running down my face, crying uncontrollably I kept asking her, WHY? WHY? Why had she hated me so? To this day, I still do not know the answer. Then I did something I hadn't expected of myself, I whispered and told her I forgave her. The Lord had to have been working through me there. Without His Love I would not have been able to forgive her, I know that. Now in all those years, she had never ever came to me and asked for my forgiveness or even told me why she had treated me that way, Now dead she looked so frail, little and shriveled up. I felt sorry for her.

While at the funeral home, my cousin Michelle, came to me speaking of her concern, apologizing on behalf of her parents. She explained she had no idea why they did not become involved throughout the years of abuse I had suffered. Michelle, a Guidance Counselor herself, had heard a lot of terrible horror stories of abuse from her school children, but she never knew the details and extent of the abuse I had endured. Her parents, Uncle Al and Aunt Kit knew of some of the abuse, but they never took any steps to help.

On the way home from the funeral, I kept saying. "I feel FREE, I feel FREE", like I was a bird just let out of its cage. Here I was a grown woman with children and grandchildren. I still had this fear of her, but the fear was gone. I felt a heavy weight fall off my shoulders. I was as light as a feather. What I had feared all those years was finally gone.

Then two weeks after the funeral, I was so upset I stayed in tears and was unable to eat or sleep. I felt so guilty. Finally, I had a consultation with my pastor, Brother Rodney. He advised me I had nothing to feel guilty for. If anyone should have felt guilty, it should have been my Aunt. He explained that every time I looked back on my childhood, there were so many unhappy and unpleasant memories. Fear was such a big part of my life it consumed me; this is why I felt it for so long. To tell the truth, I never wanted anyone to die, but I was glad when she did. I felt guilty for thinking that way. I asked the Lord to help me overcome and I begged for his forgiveness.

**Ephesians 4:32 "And be ye kind one to another, tenderhearted forgiving one another."**

# <u>Chapter 31 "Starting Over"</u>

I have started over again by myself. All my children are married, but by the grace of God I have made it. I have a job, have bought my mobile home, and getting on with my life. I still live in the country, not far from the farm, and am a member of the Broadlands Bible Church. I could have become quite bitter throughout the years, but with the Lord's help, I've over come most of the obstacles that have come my way. I have found peace. Over the years we have made many precious dear friends and wonderful neighbors: the Crains, Reeves, Schmidts, Deckers, Classens, Kahns, Joneses, Smiths, Bertrands, Travises, Rectors, Shirleys, and the Moses, just to mention a few families. There are so many, I would not trade them or the community where I live for any other place on earth.

My eldest daughter, Therese May, and her husband Tim have been married for over twenty-two years now. They have blessed me with two beautiful precious grandchildren. Their son, Nathan, is a Louisiana Forester. He is married to Jodi, and they have blessed me with a little great-grand son, little Nate. Nathan loves the woods, the out of doors, loves to either be fishing or hunting. He is our Daniel Boone. Their daughter Rebecca is 19 years old and is searching for her place in life. She is a beautiful girl, and has the most beautiful eyes. (I'm not bragging, just stating a fact). While in high school she loved sports, playing softball and basketball. Therese May is the secretary for our fire department here in our small country town. Therese favors my husband's side of the family with blondish/brown hair and green eyes. After graduating from high school, twenty years later she graduated from College, I am very proud of her. Tim is a superintendent for a construction company in Lake Charles. They attend church and Sunday School regularly. Tim sings with a gospel group, "The Sanctuary Quartet."

My son Billy Joe and his wife Tina have been married for about 11 years. They also have blessed me with two precious grandchildren Ty is 10 years old. He likes to play baseball and football and loves to ride his four-wheeler. Their youngest Hayden is 3 years old, and is a bundle of energy. He is almost too pretty to be a boy, with curly blond hair. Hayden favors Tina's side of the family. Working in the woods from daylight until dark, Billy Joe drives an eighteen-wheeler just like his father and grandfather before him. Instead of hauling milk, he hauls wood (logs) to the Boise Paper Mill and surrounding paper mills. He favors my side of the family with brown eyes and brown hair. Ty is the image of his Daddy. They also attend church and Sunday school regularly, and Billy Joe sings in the choir. Often, I refer to Billy Joe as my "Baby Huey". He's so tall and big and I'm so short and little. I bought him the comic book so he would know who "Baby Huey" is.

My youngest daughter, Donna Dee, and her husband Clint, have been married for 6 ½ years. They have also blessed me with two precious beautiful grandchildren. Shelby is 6 years old and in kindergarten. She's cute as a button and thinks she's all grown up. She plays T-Ball during the summer months and has taken swimming lessons. Wesley is 3 years old and a hand full! He loves riding on the four-wheeler also. Donna favors my side of the family with the brown eyes and dark brown hair. Clint works for an offshore company on a land oil rig. They both are volunteer firefighters for our little community. They also attend church and Sunday School regularly. All of my children live close by. I am proud of each of my children; they are very special and precious to me. Each of my grandchildren and great-grandchild are unique in their own special way.

**Proverbs 3:5 "Trust in the Lord with all thine heart and lean not unto thine own understanding."**

# Chapter 32 "Conclusion"

I have written this story because I felt the need to make others aware that we abused children do not always become abusive parents. My sister and I certainly are not. Rose, nor I grew up to become juvenile delinquents, murders, robbers, nor a burden to the state. We have both held jobs working most all of our lives. Both of us have raised wholesome children who have earned their own way in life.

As I've stated before, my abuser rarely beat my sister, I received all the beatings and lashings for the both of us. Rose asked me not too long ago if I hated her for all that had taken place in our lives. She felt the blame, suffering mental and emotional deprivation. I explained to her that she was only a child too, and there was nothing she could have done to prevent it. This was beyond our control. No, I didn't hate her then or now. She is my sister, the only one with whom I felt safe. I thank the Lord for her, for standing by me throughout this terrible ordeal. Now she wants the past to say in the past. She does not want to relate to any of it still to this day. She says it still hurts too much to remember it all.

We were two little girls brought up in an environment of fear and treated like prisoners in our own home. Where we should have been enjoying our childhood, we feared it. Ours is a memory of nightmares. We were unhappy, insecure, and frustrated most of the time. We totally turned our lives over to the Lord and prayed for deliverance.

I realize I have said this before, and I am saying it again: not ALL abused children become abusive parents. I imagine there are a lot of us out there. I'm not saying we weren't strict raising our children, but we NEVER ABUSED them. In fact I believe we were overly protective of them and loved them far more then we love ourselves. Probably we love them for all the years we weren't loved. We give our children grandchildren and great-grandchildren all the love we have. To me children are the most precious gifts God can bestow upon us.

People who are acquainted with me today say they can hardly believe I was abused when I was a child. While employed at our local hospital I came in contact with children who were abused by their parents or relatives. In conversations with my co-workers they voiced their outrage about how they can't understand anyone being so cruel to his or her own child. When I first began to open up and share bits and pieces of my experiences with them, to let them know I could identify with the child, they would say they had never met anyone who had been abused. They would say, to see me, talk with me, and know me, as I am today made it hard for them to understand why I was so mistreated. They wondered why my sister or I didn't rob stores, become criminals, do drugs, or get angry to let out our frustrations. These kinds of notions never entered our minds. The scars are on the inside, not the outside.

It has been said that in order to love you must first have experienced being loved. I know we were starved for love, as we certainly never received any. To have been an abused child and turn into an abusive parent to me is a cop out. Surely the abused person must know abusing their children is not the best way. An abused person can turn their lives around and make their life better for themselves and their children.

I became a volunteer involved with a program called "Welcome Home". It counseled and taught new mothers in the caring and raising of their children from infancy into teen years. As a lot of new mothers really don't know what's ahead for them. The program helps them face the day-to-day problems that might come up in their lives. It also gave the mothers advice on handling stressful situations. We handed them brochures, offered tapes for them to borrow, and checked out booklets for them. If I have helped one mother learn to love, nourish and care for her child, it's been a worthwhile experience for me. Also, I am involved with our local chapter of Child Abuse Awareness of Louisiana.

The only way I have been able to deal with all of this through the years has been by holding onto the Lord's hand and letting him lead me. Through answered prayers, he has helped me overcome these terribly trying situations. He has shown me how to love and be loved, to continue on with whatever is ahead in life. I am very grateful for my faith in God.

Abuse is an awful cycle, but it can be broken by power of God. I have turned my life around with God's guidance and strength. He blessed me with a wonderful husband and three wonderful children. Now I am blessed with grandchildren and great-grandchildren. It was not by my doings alone, but by his I have come this far. I give all the praise and glory to my Saviour, Jesus Christ.

**Psalms 33:21 "For our hearts shall rejoice in him, because we have trusted in His Holy Name."**

Some names have been changed to protect the privacy of those still living.

Written by Esther J. Mathis

*Esther J. Mathis*

# **Friendship**

Definition of a friend according to Webster: One who is attached by affection, one who has esteem and regard for another. This describes Joe'l Mathis and what she has been to me for many years.

I have known Joe'l for thirty-four years and she has been a true friend from the day we met and she will be my friend for life. We have shared so many times together, good and bad. During the good times we laughed and celebrated together. Through the bad, we cried, counseled, and tried to comfort one another.

There have been many bad times in Joe'l's life. I know that it started at a very young age. In spite of the neglect and abuse she received as a child, Joe'l overcame that sad childhood. She became a warm, loving, and caring person. She was a good and loving wife to her husband. Joe'l supported him in his decisions in life and was there for him until the day his life ended. Their marriage had ups and downs, as all marriages do. But her faith in God and her loyalty to her husband always prevailed.

Her children are blessed to have her as their mother, two of them exceptionally so. Because they received her love as adopted children. However, seeing her with all her children, one would not know which are adopted. She loves and treats them all the same.

Joe'l is known and loved by many people. When her name is mentioned within a conversation, nothing but nice things is ever said concerning her. Which is the only way it could be. There is only good about Joe'l.

A Dear Friend,
**Francis Bertrand**

This is a true autobiography about the life of an abused child, growing up just after the depression years. The reader will see how the author deals with emotional and physical abuse.

Because their Mother died young, and their father could not care for them, Joe'l and her sister, Rose, were shifted from one home to another until finally, an Aunt agreed to take them in.

This book will take you through terrifying years of the authors' youth and allow you to witness first-hand the cruel and awful effects of child-abuse. It will lead you out of the abusive system and into the adult life of Joe'l. It will show that an abused child can overcome tremendous obstacles and blossom into a loving, caring wife and mother without fulfilling the expectation that they have not succumbed to becoming abusive parents. "No Place to Run, No Place to Hide"; will fill you with fear, horrify you the graphic details, and slowly turn your heart with the triumphant outcome.

**Author (in white) and Sister**

# About the Author

Esther "Joe'l" Mathis was born in 1938 in New Orleans, La. She has one sister; Rose. Their mother passed away when Joe'l was only three, shortly after this they were adopted by an aunt and moved to Chicago. Joe'l & Rose moved back to New Orleans in 1954 where she met her husband of 31 years, DeWitt, in 1956, and moved to DeRidder, LA in 1957.

They have two daughters and one son. Joe'l now enjoys the addition of seven grandchildren, two great grandsons, and a great granddaughter on the way. She is a member of Broadlands Bible Church. A member of Louisiana Council of Child Abuse. Joe'l enjoys spending time with her family and friends. She is also a member of the First Baptist Church Singles Group, where she enjoys weekly fellowship activities with the group.

Printed in the United States
1324200004B/498